T0358195

Cambridge Elements

Elements in Leadership
edited by
Ronald E. Riggio
Claremont McKenna College
Susan E. Murphy
University of Edinburgh

Founding Editor
Georgia Sorenson
University of Cambridge

THE GIFT OF TRANSFORMATIVE LEADERS

Nathan O. Hatch
Wake Forest University

CAMBRIDGE
UNIVERSITY PRESS

Shaftesbury Road, Cambridge CB2 8EA, United Kingdom

One Liberty Plaza, 20th Floor, New York, NY 10006, USA

477 Williamstown Road, Port Melbourne, VIC 3207, Australia

314–321, 3rd Floor, Plot 3, Splendor Forum, Jasola District Centre,
New Delhi – 110025, India

103 Penang Road, #05–06/07, Visioncrest Commercial, Singapore 238467

Cambridge University Press is part of Cambridge University Press & Assessment,
a department of the University of Cambridge.

We share the University's mission to contribute to society through the pursuit of
education, learning and research at the highest international levels of excellence.

www.cambridge.org
Information on this title: www.cambridge.org/9781009517355

DOI: 10.1017/9781009405072

First published 2024

A catalogue record for this publication is available from the British Library.

ISBN 978-1-009-51735-5 Hardback
ISBN 978-1-009-40504-1 Paperback
ISSN 2631-7796 (online)
ISSN 2631-7788 (print)

Cambridge University Press & Assessment has no responsibility for the persistence
or accuracy of URLs for external or third-party internet websites referred to in this
publication and does not guarantee that any content on such websites is, or will
remain, accurate or appropriate.

The Gift of Transformative Leaders

Elements in Leadership

DOI: 10.1017/9781009405072
First published online: April 2024

Nathan O. Hatch
Wake Forest University

Author for correspondence: Nathan O. Hatch, hatch@wfu.edu

Abstract: Great organizations flourish in the hands of transformative leaders. Most organizations remain competitive but are unlikely to advance without impetus. Only exceptional leaders in an organization can fulfill an ambition for real institutional advancement. Drawing on the author's decades-long career in higher education, including as a former university president and provost at two top-30 national universities, this Element showcases leaders recruited and empowered by the author to advance and transform institutions. At each institution, the author witnessed pockets of mediocrity transform into national examples of excellence. Finding the right leader to spearhead the work was the key to growth and success nearly every time. Through the stories of thirteen transformative leaders, this Element illuminates how the author approached identifying talent and empowered leaders to lead in bold and creative ways.

This Element also has a video abstract: www.cambridge.org/CELE_Hatch

Keywords: leadership, transformation, teamwork, recruiting, character

ISBNs: 9781009517355 (HB), 9781009405041 (PB), 9781009405072 (OC)
ISSNs: 2631-7796 (online), 2631-7788 (print)

Contents

Nathan O. Hatch

Introduction

Great organizations flourish at the hands of transformative leaders. Most organizations stay more or less the way they are – stable, competitive at their level, but unlikely to move dramatically forward – without significant and unusual impetus. Only exceptional leaders, spread throughout an organization, can fulfill an ambition for real institutional advance. Great leaders are a marvelous gift.

Most books on leadership assume it is the animating presence of the CEO that drives success. This Element suggests a different path – a CEO willing to gather a team talented enough to take on transformation as a joint project. In the process of institutional transformation, those leaders surrounding a chief executive are just as important as the top leader – if that senior team is unleashed and empowered to be transformative in their respective spheres.

It is a given that CEOs across education, business, government, medicine, and nonprofits are very skilled, but they are not equipped with every talent set needed to lead effective and transformational change across their organizations. In order to expand that capacity for transformation, CEOs must seek, support, and set the vision for talented leaders. Complex organizations cannot sustain long-term success if all of the energy and control radiates from the center.

This means that leading from the top will have to be unconventional. A good hire, one leader has said, always makes one reinvent oneself. Leading gifted leaders is far more challenging – and exhilarating – and requires the CEO to resist the impulse to control. They must grant to others throughout the organization the space – the elbow room – to take charge, to innovate, and to expand their own horizons. In a time when many people are threatened by leaders who possess skills they lack, this Element illustrates what defines transformative leaders and why organizations should be clamoring for them.

In my forty years in higher education, including stints as a university president and provost at two top-30 universities, I worked with some incredible leaders whose stories of transformation are in the following pages. Because of them, both the University of Notre Dame and Wake Forest University developed grander visions, broader appeal, greater resources, and increased clarification of their distinct missions. At each institution, I witnessed pockets of mediocrity transform into national examples of excellence. Finding the right leader to spearhead the work was the key to growth and success nearly every time.

In the following profiles, you will see how critical it was to identify talent better than oneself, embrace unconventional recruiting and hiring, empower leaders to lead in bold and creative ways, learn from those with expertise, and take talent and turn it into teams.

Identifying Talent Better than Oneself

Most executives give lip service to hiring talent better than themselves – a practice that is usually the exception rather than the rule. The hunt for talent requires a constant eye on the horizon. It means having a pulse on what areas of the organization could benefit from transformative leadership and who – in and out of the industry – is making real advancements in a specific space. Hunting for talent necessitates a certain level of curiosity about potential within the organization and potential in people. It is also a process built on patience and observation. And the patient and consistent scouring for talent is not to be underestimated. Often, the best candidate isn't one who submitted an application when a certain position became available; sometimes it is a leader you've been observing and watching for a long time.

Embracing Unconventional Recruiting and Hiring

When an executive looks to hire, most recruiting is done in conventional and predictable ways. Positions are filled with perfectly acceptable candidates, but not those who will change the trajectory of an institution. Most hiring is done to fulfill a conventional position description, not to raise the bar, expand the vision, or reach for a new level of excellence.

Sometimes unconventional recruitment and hiring are needed to convince a leader to join the team. Instead of relying solely on search firms, I took on some of the work – going to great lengths to meet with people, listening to how they wanted to invest their careers, gaining keen insight into their motivations as a whole person, and crafting opportunities for the institution and community to benefit most from the individual. Spending time with potential leaders provided an opportunity to get to know them and their families to ensure that it would be a good fit for everyone.

During one search, I met with ten people without finding the leader I knew was needed. So, I paused the search, and I waited until I found a leader who was able to transform that area of the university. During another search, the candidate made it clear that relocating to North Carolina would be a family decision. So, we invited the candidate's children to campus and personally invested in how they could become part of the community. And, more than once, I worked to clear away obstacles, including altering a given position to align with a leader's gifts and talents.

Empowering Leaders to Lead in Bold and Creative Ways

A compelling vision – one with meaning and purpose – is what motivates the most talented of leaders. That meant I had to think very intentionally about what was asked and expected of a leader. Personal ambition on the part of leaders often correlated with institutional ambition. Even as they used the best of their talent, creativity, and innovation, they aligned it with the mission of the institution.

Empowering leaders means allowing them to think expansively about the promise of their role, understanding their hopes and dreams, giving them appropriate autonomy in how to achieve their goals, and standing beside them with the necessary financial resources.

If leaders want to recruit some of the finest talent, they must be ready to empower the dreams and vision of their hires. Allowing the space to imagine and create while providing the appropriate support will enable and encourage institutional transformation.

Learning from Those with Expertise

Leading a team of high talent became a learning laboratory for me over two decades. As a university president, I was leading a team of not only academic leaders but also those across the diverse spectrum of the modern university – in finance and administration, athletics, investments, development, and health care. I often questioned how to refocus my own leadership style to permit these leaders to flourish for the good of the institution. Over time, I learned at least three important lessons about how to lead when you are surrounded by colleagues more talented than yourself.

First, I learned how to be challenged – understanding that the leader does not always have the best answer or idea. When it came to discussions of finance, development, athletics, medicine, or student affairs, I was usually not the most knowledgeable in the room. Others had spent years immersed in those respective fields. Chief executives cultivate a climate where leaders can have open, honest, and sometimes challenging discussions. To succeed, a leader does not always have to be right.

Second, I learned the values of distributed leadership. The leader sets the tone for the whole organization – its identity and aspiration. But equally important is a leader's role in supporting and running interference for the good ideas and plans of others. The university was best served if many aspirational leaders were building dynamic programs, brainstorming together, and dreaming of what was possible.

Third, I came to understand that gifted leaders stretch the executive's own leadership capacity. Hiring gifted people keeps a leader on their toes, forcing executives to strengthen their own leadership. I had to plan creatively and work hard to build trust and confidence among leaders.

Leading and Managing

Warren Bennis (1990), in *On Becoming a Leader*, distinguished management and leadership, suggesting that managers do things the right way while leaders do the right things. In the profiles that follow, I am impressed that these leaders do not make such a sharp differentiation between these roles. They focus on the most important things to do but also give great attention to how things get done – vision and implementation.

At Notre Dame and Wake Forest, I was blessed to work with many great leaders not included in these profiles. Many faculty, staff, and administrators deserve credit for the success of these institutions. I profiled these thirteen individuals because, with one exception, I was involved in recruiting them and privileged to observe, up close, their transformative work.

Profiling this set of leaders is worthy in its own right. What they accomplished and how they went about their work are stories worth telling. Beyond that, I am convinced that it is valuable to examine exemplary leaders, particularly at a time when cynicism abounds about leaders and institutions. Exemplars can inspire, provide guidance in how to act in given situations, be powerful reminders of our values, and provide evidence that specific ideals can be realized (Brant, Brooks, & Lamb, 2022). All of us, in whatever professional context, can learn from the way these leaders, each in their own way, took up the challenges of their day. Their stories can then serve as a gift to students of leadership far beyond the institutions they worked to transform.

1 What Is Transformative Leadership?

I have been privileged to work with some remarkable leaders. Their leadership covers a broad range of areas, from the liberal arts to medicine, from coaching and athletics to fundraising, from financial administration to character development. These leaders are widely different in style and personality: extraverts and introverts, serious and jocular, emotional and calm, sophisticated and plain-spoken. Some pursued the same vocational path their whole career; others made radical shifts. They are very different people, and they lead in vastly different styles.

What common threads can one find in examining these thirteen leaders? What, in short, constitutes transformative leadership? In the profiles that follow, I detect several distinct characteristics or common threads evident in the work of these colleagues.

Frank Assessment

The first theme is that of honesty and transparency about an organization. Transformative leaders must have the courage to admit reality and call out what is excellent and what is mediocre. Too many leaders and organizations are mired in a mindset of success and speak of their group as excellent when, by any objective measure, they are only average. Transformative leaders push organizations not to be self-referential. They instinctively compare with the best and are not afraid to call on their peers to admit shortcomings and strive for improvement. They welcome frank assessment.

In this task, I have found transformative leaders to be both lovers and critics. They both admire and value the organization of which they are a part – and are perceived as having that affection – yet they also sustain a critical eye – providing realistic and comparative assessments. They esteem what has gone before, valuing tradition; but they are not satisfied with traditional modes that fall short of excellence.

The Blue Flame of Ambition

Transformative leaders have a blue flame of ambition. They are restless to accomplish. They measure themselves by specific achievement. They love their work and turn their most creative energies to it – often morning, noon, and night. They have a big engine.

It was said of Abraham Lincoln that his ambition was a little engine that knew no rest. Through thick and thin, amid many failures and disappointments, he had an abiding drive to accomplish things. In 1841, the melancholy Lincoln, doubting whether his life would amount to anything, confessed to a friend, "I would be more than willing to die, except that I have done nothing to make any human remember that I have lived" (Goodwin, 2005, p. 99).

The best leaders have learned to channel this innate ambition to serve larger purposes, the organization they are called upon to lead. Writer Jim Collins has noted that this kind of "humility" is one of the two central characteristics he found in leaders and companies that succeed over a long time. The transformative leaders I study in this Element all have considerable ambition, but all have shown far more concern about institutional success than personal advancement (Collins, 2001).

Vision

Great leaders couple ambition to a distinct vision for the future. They can stand overlooking a vista and imagine a future that others may not see – a courageous heart for the horizon. This kind of imagination, applied to real life circumstances, is a special gift. Grounded in reality, it must provide convincing motivation that can capture the hearts and minds of an organization.

Transformative leaders are driven principally by a sense of mission. The real driver in their life – and what usually convinces them to take one job over another – is a powerful sense of mission. Collins notes this in his monograph on leadership in the social sectors. What leaders find compelling, he notes, are those things that have an inherent power to ignite passion and commitment: "Educating young people, connecting people to God, making our cities safe, touching the soul with great art, feeding the hungry, serving the poor, or protecting our freedom" (Collins, 2001, p. 16).

Opportunistic Strategy and Risk

In *Richard III*, William Shakespeare noted that "Talkers are no good doers; be assur'd we come to use our hands and not our tongues" (Folger Shakespeare Library, n.d.). A convincing vision is not enough for real transformative leadership. The clutch must be engaged. Real plans must be put into place. Visions can only be achieved when incremental steps are taken in a given direction. What path is to be taken and which paths avoided?

Leaders I have known thought about strategy in two distinct ways. First, they were not afraid to chart paths that were distinct and exceptional. There is no strategy, someone has said, if you and the competitors are doing exactly the same thing. Transformational leaders also realize that the best strategists are poised to seize opportunities. Professor and administrator John Lombardi once noted that the most successful universities are those that have a sixth sense for opportunities, ready to open the door even as the knock is heard (Lombardi et al., 2000). Strategy means applying a vision to the concrete here and now.

To seize opportunity is often to take risks. It requires a measure of courage to move beyond what is conventional and expected. All of the leaders profiled in this Element were never afraid to launch new programs, invite new partners, imagine new facilities, and redesign organizations. They repeatedly chose opportunity over safety, future possibilities over the tried and true. They had the courage and confidence to take risks.

Resolve

Both a dream and real plans are necessary for change. All of the leaders profiled here also share a mindset of persistence and determination. They have vision and seize opportunities. But they also take up the tasks, day by day, with a relentless work ethic. They explore every lead, make the extra phone call, and go out of their way to build coalitions, particularly with those with whom they have disagreements. They are steady in their purpose and diligent in carrying it out. Studying their work habits up close, I am reminded of the brilliant inventor Louis Pasteur, who claimed, "My strength lies solely in my tenacity" (Pasteur & Vallery-Radot, 1939).

These leaders lean into disappointment and setback. They are not daunted by obstacles and rather adjust and recalibrate to changing conditions. They possess that ingredient of success that psychologist Angela Duckworth has called "grit" – powerful, long-term perseverance, through thick and thin. The fear of failure does not deter them from taking risks, even from making big bets (Duckworth, 2016).

Self-Knowledge and Emotional Intelligence

There are certain things, like oxygen, that become most noticeable by their absence. All of us can think of instances where leaders of great talent stumble in their new responsibilities because they fail to read the people and organizations they are called upon to lead. They do not sense how they are coming across or whether their presence is generating trust or resistance. They stride into situations without calibrating the impact of their own force field, or they do not take the time to know the people they are trying to lead. They lack both self-knowledge and emotional intelligence.

This quality of being able to calibrate one's leadership in altered circumstances is harder to detect than stronger qualities such as ambition and vision – which can be easily detected in interviews and conversation. Listening well and plumbing the depths of institutional culture are equally important but more latent gifts. Strong leadership will be thwarted if people choose not to follow.

Psychologist Daniel Goleman first brought the term "emotional intelligence" to a wider audience in his 1995 classic article in the *Harvard Business Review*. Goleman, following the original research by Peter Salovey, now president of Yale University, argues that qualities of emotional intelligence are the sine qua non of leadership – more important than intelligence, toughness, determination, and vision (Goleman, 1995; Goleman, 2004).

By emotional intelligence, he refers to qualities such as self-awareness, self-regulation, motivation, empathy, and social skills. When he calculated these against ingredients of excellent performance such as technical skills and IQ, emotional intelligence proved to be twice as important for jobs at all levels. Moreover, his analysis showed that emotional intelligence played an increasingly important role at the highest levels of management. Two hallmarks of this kind of awareness are a self-deprecating sense of humor and a thirst for constructive criticism.

The effective leaders I have known all have been blessed with ample measures of emotional intelligence. They are adept in comprehending and responding to the culture of the organization they are called to lead. They call for change and action in ways that are heard and understood by their colleagues. They understand the distinction made by James MacGregor Burns in his classic *Leadership* that the practice of leadership is not the same as the exercise of power. True leadership exists if people follow when they have the freedom not to. This principle is certainly true in not-for-profit organizations but also in business, where executives don't have the same concentration of pure executive power they once enjoyed (Collins, 2005).

Trust and Mutual Empowerment

There is growing interest in thinking about leadership as a relationship (Burns, 1978). Are interactions merely instrumental or deeply relational and empowering – where leaders take followers seriously and inspire them in ways that build trust? Studies increasingly point to trust as the most reliable measure of executive performance. All of a leader's vaunted ambition, vision, or strategy will go for naught if people around them come to doubt one's integrity and character. Frances X. Frei and Anne Morriss describe three simple drivers of trust: authenticity (*I experience the real you*); logic (*Your judgment is sound*); and empathy (*I believe you care about my success*) (Frei & Morriss, 2020). Great leaders, it can be shown, are people who can be trusted.

One thing that leaders often overlook is that people in an organization are shrewd and can detect what is real and what is feigned or false. People can detect hypocrisy. They can see through veneers of niceness. They can tell when they are being manipulated or outsmarted (The Arbinger Institute, 2018). Over time, a leader's real intentions and motives become evident to those who work around them, day after day.

In *Transforming Leadership*, James MacGregor Burns suggests that the finest examples of leadership involve a two-way interaction in which "the leader offers initiatives that followers pick up, amplify, reshape, and direct back onto the leader" (Burns, 2018, p. 27). A truly transformative leader liberates and empowers those with whom they work.

Character

The greatest privilege of my professional life has been to work with a set of leaders whose work has been transformative – and to realize, in each case, that gift is related to character. In their own distinct way, each of these leaders has been able to foster an atmosphere of trust. They have shown authenticity, empathy, and sound judgment even as they moved an organization in significantly new directions. These leaders operated out of a deep set of values. They were true to their word, they treated people with respect, and they made decisions on behalf of the common good.

At the end of the day, it is heartening to realize that trust and character are at the very heart of transformative leadership. Doing things the right way, and treating people the right way, define the clearest path to real and lasting success.

Carolyn Woo

2 Carolyn Woo: Harnessing Ambition to Better the World

Carolyn is this force of nature. She's incredibly brilliant and insightful, and she believes in a vision for making the world a better place.

Michele Broemmelsiek
Vice President, Overseas Operations at Catholic Relief Services

I was fascinated from the moment I met Carolyn Woo. She had grown up in Hong Kong in the 1950s and 1960s with strong Confucian and Catholic influences. She defied her father's – and her culture's – expectations simply to "marry well," instead raising money from her siblings to come to the United States for a college education as her brothers had done. She had enough for one year of tuition and room and board. In 1972, she became a star student at Purdue University and won scholarships for her bachelor's degree, master's degree in business, and doctorate in strategic management (University of Notre Dame, n.d.).

When I first met Carolyn, she was a high-level administrator at Purdue. Previously, she had been a professor of strategic management and directed Purdue's MBA program when it moved dramatically into the top 25 programs in the nation.

In the summer of 1996, I was a new provost at Notre Dame looking for a dean for the Mendoza College of Business. Someone told me about Carolyn and her expertise in strategic management. Her professional accomplishments made it obvious to me that she was most successful when she merged her vocation and her faith – making sure that business was used as a force for good in the world.

Feeling that she would be an outstanding candidate to lead business education at Notre Dame, I drove from South Bend to West Lafayette, Indiana, and met her at a restaurant off campus. From the start, she said she was not interested in being a candidate for the Notre Dame position, and our meeting off campus underscored there was nothing official about this visit.

During the conversation, Carolyn's energy, vision, and striking blend of ambition and humility clearly struck me. She knew her mind, she understood management education, and she thought brilliantly about strategy. Carolyn sustained strong personal relationships with colleagues, friends, and family, and she had a deep moral commitment to accomplish big and important things for the common good.

What also became clear in that first conversation was that Carolyn was fiercely loyal to Purdue and her colleagues there. Purdue had become her home in a deep and powerful way. The university had provided scholarships for her education, and friends in that community had nurtured her from her days as a lonely and insecure student. She met her husband, David, at the St. Thomas Aquinas Center on campus, and that community remained a vital part of their lives. Now, she had the rare experience of working with senior leaders to guide the future direction of the university. She loved what she was doing, as did her husband. Their two sons, Justin and Ryan, entering their teenage years, loved Boilermaker football and everything about life in the Purdue community.

At the end of the conversation, she simply told me, "I have no reason to leave Purdue."

Driving back to South Bend, I wavered between dreaming about Carolyn's transformative potential and admitting to myself that Purdue would be her ongoing home. Ultimately, I believed it was worth the long shot to continue our conversations.

"Nathan kept sending me materials on the school, and this signaled strong interest and trust," remembered Carolyn. "He knew there was no desire on my part to leave Purdue, but he just did not go away. He was persistent. And he was patient."

For weeks, Carolyn continued to decline Notre Dame's invitation, but she never fully slammed the door. I continued the conversation, and one day, by her own telling, it dawned on her that something had changed.

"I walked out of daily mass at Purdue one day, and said, 'I think I'm staying here for the wrong reasons,'" she remembered. "'There is a task and a mission that has my name on it. That's what I need to do.' I called Nathan and told him, 'I think I will come.' I didn't even discuss terms."

In the end, the dream of a great Catholic business school fired her imagination. Carolyn agreed to stand before the School of Business faculty as the sole candidate – a potentially controversial decision for the search committee and for me. But we took the risk, not letting process get in the way of the chance to recruit an exceptional leader. There were many conversations with faculty along the way and, in the end, Carolyn was welcomed enthusiastically by the business faculty.

"It was because Nathan was able to articulate the salient factor that got me to leave Purdue: It was about [the] mission of a Catholic business school, and that came through. It was not just a recruiting line; it was communicated with sincerity and commitment," said Carolyn. "Nathan saw something that I had not realized was important: the integration of my faith in my profession."

Carolyn arrived at Notre Dame in 1997, and her impact on the Mendoza College was immediate. Because she found a deeper calling and purpose for her own vocation, she was able to spread that enthusiasm and drive and ultimately transform business education.

"You can't talk about Carolyn without talking about faith," said Bill Nichols, a colleague of Carolyn's and professor emeritus of accountancy at the Mendoza College of Business. "Her faith is so important, and as a leader, I think people respected her because of that. She likes to see people that have a meaning in life bigger than their own self-interest."

Early on, she energized a dispirited faculty, provided new resources, galvanized new projects, and set new standards. She argued strongly with me that faculty had to have more resources. One afternoon, as she was noting the lack of faculty discretionary funding, she looked at me and said, "My children have no shoes!" She was tough, mirroring to me and the university what kind of support a first-rate management program required, and she was strategic, setting forth direct plans for how an expansion of programs could enliven the school and enhance its financial position.

Through those efforts, she developed deep trust from her faculty. She was also innovative in her strategy to move the business enterprise forward – developing a revenue-sharing arrangement that would bolster the MBA program. Under her leadership, the Mendoza College prospered and with that came national recognition – including being ranked number one in undergraduate business education by *Bloomberg Businessweek* (Elliot, 2010).

Among her great gifts was building a vital academic community. She valued people – students, staff, and faculty – and nurtured a wonderful sense of community in the Mendoza College. Her deep ambitions and affection for the school animated the whole.

Carolyn went on to become a transformative leader at Notre Dame and far beyond. She was elected as the first female chair of the Association to Advance

Collegiate Schools of Business International and led the launch of the United Nations Principles for Responsible Management program. In 2012, Carolyn left Notre Dame and became the CEO of Catholic Relief Services, a humanitarian relief agency with more than 8,000 employees in over 100 countries serving over 100 million people each year. For her work in that position, *Foreign Policy* magazine named her one of thirty-one world leaders working as "a force for good" in 2013.

What I Learned

Because of Carolyn, I learned several crucial lessons about *recruitment*. While I knew the importance of good leadership, I witnessed firsthand how the right leader could transform an organization in a remarkably short time. Trust and confidence in the right leader can change outlooks and motivations across the board. And, to their credit, the Mendoza College community welcomed the clarion call for change that Carolyn set forth.

I also learned that *a compelling vision is what motivates most talented leaders* – more than prestige or financial reward. They want to give themselves to something that seems important – something that can make a difference. An essential part of recruiting is helping a candidate see those possibilities and giving them confidence that they can translate that dream into reality.

Another lesson I learned was that *working with talented leaders is demanding.* In the early years, my meetings with Carolyn were challenging. She argued forcefully about what the college needed, challenged the centralized financial modeling of the university, and spoke her mind regularly about what Notre Dame needed to do to become a great research university. These conversations challenged me to modify my own style of leadership and view of what was best for Notre Dame. I became a learner as much as a teacher. Carolyn helped me see the kind of support I needed to offer if a dean was to be transformative.

Carolyn's story also illustrates how *personal ambition correlates with institutional ambition*. Carolyn did not start at the top of American academic life. She came to America penniless and struggling to improve her English. She was desperate to prove to herself and her father that she could measure up.

Carolyn's drive to succeed, and to do so with meaning and purpose, extended to the organizations she led. She was never content with the status quo, and she was always asking not just what an organization should do, but why and for what reason. Life for her had rich meaning, bound up in how others were treated and how good purposes were achieved. It is an aura she naturally infused into her professional life at Purdue University, the University of Notre Dame, and Catholic Relief Services.

John Affleck-Graves

3 John Affleck-Graves: Renewing an Organization by Investing in Its People

John Affleck-Graves is key to why Notre Dame is universally respected for its superb management by institutional leaders across the country.

John J. Brennan
Chair, Board of Trustees, University of Notre Dame
(Observer Staff Report, 2018)

I set my sights on John Affleck-Graves as Carolyn Woo's successor as dean of the Mendoza College of Business at Notre Dame. He was the complete package. He was a captivating finance professor, winner of six teaching awards at Notre Dame and two at the University of Cape Town in South Africa. According to lore, toward the end of his teaching career at Notre Dame, he won the teaching award nearly every year. Repeatedly, he turned it down, hoping instead a younger faculty member would receive the recognition.

For three years, from 1997 until 2000, he chaired Notre Dame's finance and business economics department brilliantly, adding outstanding faculty, and building morale and momentum. A distinguished scholar and great public speaker, he often made presentations to university donors, parents, and friends.

More than anything, John was creative. Working with the endowment office at Notre Dame, he was instrumental in launching the Applied Investment Management (AIM) program that has since become legendary. Created in 1995, the course offered thirty finance majors a two-semester experience in live portfolio management while developing analysis skills through rigorous, fundamental equity research. Students manage a fund – currently valued at $28 million – and present their decisions to the AIM Advisory Board, a select group of active investment professionals. Over 1,200 students have graduated from this program, which virtually assured them an analyst position in a Wall Street firm.

John and his wife, Rita, were also people of great character. Their lives had not been easy. They grew up and were educated in Cape Town, South Africa. John earned a doctorate in mathematical statistics and taught both mathematics and finance at the University of Cape Town. In the mid-1980s, with apartheid still a discouraging reality in South Africa, John and Rita made the decision of conscience to immigrate to the United States. This choice came with considerable professional sacrifice. A full professor at the University of Cape Town, John had to relaunch his career in the United States, starting over as an assistant professor of finance at Notre Dame. With resolve and infectious goodwill, John took on every challenge set before him, becoming one of Notre Dame's most valuable members of the faculty.

In the summer of 2000, I was vacationing with my family in London when I received a call from the office to say that, after fourteen years at Notre Dame, John had accepted a position at Florida State University as the Patty Hill Smith Eminent Scholar in Finance. I was shocked and bewildered.

When I spoke with John, he was burned out trying to balance excellence in teaching, research, and administration all at the same time. Florida State offered a position without formal responsibility. He could teach and write in whatever ways he chose. A second reason had to do with climate. Having grown up in Cape Town, John and Rita were accustomed to warm and inviting weather. South Bend winters offered neither.

For a few months, I accepted the inevitable and moved on. But I could never quite get John out of my mind. He was so gifted and well suited for the mission of Notre Dame. So, one day, with a devilish brainstorm, I simply picked up the phone and called him. Would he consider returning to Notre Dame as vice president and associate provost, handling fiscal matters for academic life at Notre Dame? To my delight, he called back in a couple of days and said, for reasons of mission and purpose, he and Rita decided they would accept an offer to return to Notre Dame.

In 2001, a year after he left, John returned to Notre Dame as vice president and associate provost, and for three years, we were privileged to work together (Gebhard, 2019). He shrewdly managed the financial structure of academic life at Notre Dame and, more importantly, took on a raft of special projects: renewing the structure and purpose of the faculty senate, restructuring the economics department to academic distinction, and playing a crucial role in strategic planning. He was a great thought partner and trusted confidant who helped to build an engaging – and fun – team in the provost's office. As an officer of the university, he made signal contributions to the broader university – something taken note of by President Father John Jenkins and the trustees.

In 2004, Notre Dame searched for a new executive vice president and turned to John, an academic, to assume the position. To have a faculty member appointed as the university's chief financial officer was unprecedented, but clear evidence of John's sterling abilities and reputation.

Over the next fifteen years, John served with distinction as the university's chief financial officer, managing the operating budget, the endowment, human resources, information technology, construction, and other business affairs. In this senior role, John made significant contributions in at least four areas.

First, he brought the finest business acumen to the task of building a great university. With another terrific leader, Provost Thomas G. Burish, he created the Advancing Our Vision initiative in 2011, which identified and implemented financial efficiencies that gave the university new funds for academic investment, including creating eighty new faculty lines (Gebhard, 2019; Jenkins, 2011).

He also shrewdly managed the financial structure of the university. During his tenure, the operating budget of the university grew from $650 million to $1.5 billion and the endowment increased from $3.5 billion to $13 billion (Gebhard, 2019). John ensured there were no sleepy corners in the university's financial and administrative operations. He compared units with the best in class and relished bringing innovative solutions to traditional operations.

Secondly, John shepherded the greatest expansion and modernization of Notre Dame's physical plant in its history, adding thirty-six new buildings totaling 3.3 million square feet. This included the Campus Crossroads project, a $400 million investment in academic, administrative, athletic, and student space (Bauer, 2018). He also was instrumental in establishing a major endowment to provide ongoing support and maintenance of the physical campus.

Thirdly, John took the lead in helping Notre Dame invest in its local community. He chaired the Regional Development Authority (Gebhard, 2019) and played a key role in a $42 million state grant to promote economic development.

Finally, and most importantly, John made a huge commitment to investing in the 4,000 employees of Notre Dame. "Our greatest resource is our people," John said on numerous occasions (Gebhard, 2019).

"John loves talented people," said Mike Seamon, a friend and former colleague of John's. "He wanted talented people around him. He was not fearful of hiring and finding the most talented people he could. He can identify talent; he can grow talent; and he's okay with talent continuing on in their development."

John was always looking for fresh ways to make Notre Dame a better place to work – including making personal investments in those who reported to him.

"John wasn't going to micromanage," said Shannon Cullinan, a former employee of John's who now serves as the executive vice president of Notre Dame. "He knew I wouldn't grow if he did, and that's really how young or aspiring leaders grow – by doing it. He put my growth ahead of his own."

He was an innovator in professional development opportunities – and maybe that's because he was a teacher who had a very curious mind. Over a ten-year period, the budget in that area increased twentyfold (Gebhard, 2019). "John is a mix between teacher and student," said Cullinan. "He has a curiosity that is off the charts."

His signature effort was the Leadership Rotation Program, which annually took ten emerging leaders outside of their normal responsibilities for a year and allowed them to cycle through other university units. Upon his retirement in 2019, the program was named the John Affleck-Graves Excellence in Leadership Program (Gebhard, 2019).

"I consider John one of my greatest mentors and one of my greatest friends," said Seamon. "You can't say that about too many people in your life, but with the ones you do, they are at the very top and the core of who I am."

What I Learned

John taught me that *it is wise to trust your basic instincts.* From the time I observed him as a faculty member, I had the strongest sense that he would be a formidable senior leader. Nothing I saw – his good sense of humor, his humility, his fair play in faculty discussions, his relentless hard work – suggested otherwise. I had detected in him all the essentials for senior leadership, and that was proven time and time again.

I learned, once again, that *mission is what drives leaders.* What John missed in his brief sojourn in Florida was Notre Dame's palpable sense of mission and the community that formed around it. As with Carolyn Woo, that was the pivotal issue when the vocational decision had to be made.

I also learned *how freeing it is to have close associates that excel in areas where you lack expertise.* I had no formal training or experience in finance. I think in words, not spreadsheets. John was a brilliant financial analyst and brought to the provost's office a missing analytic rigor. At the same time, he brought a sense of project management that was key in organizing an academic strategic plan. My gifts were in vision and creative program development. His were in systems and structures. These complementary gifts became the foundation for a strong team and academic advance at Notre Dame.

Lou Nanni

4 Lou Nanni: Making Everyone a Talent Scout

Lou is as inspirational a leader as I've ever seen. He is voracious about talent. He is serious about advancing the institution, and his most important decision is the next person we hire.

Shannon Cullinan
Executive Vice President, University of Notre Dame

Louis "Lou" Nanni has evolved into one of the premier fundraising professionals in America, but his journey to that end was highly improbable. When he graduated from Notre Dame in 1984, Lou worked among the poor in Santiago, Chile, teaching in a shantytown and helping build a food kitchen alongside the school for malnourished children. After earning a master's degree in international peace studies at Notre Dame in 1988 and working in economic development in the Dominican Republic, Lou took on the challenge of heading a fledgling homeless center in South Bend, Indiana (McDonald, 2016; University of Notre Dame, n.d.).

When Lou became director in 1991, it looked like so many homeless shelters – "dirty, dangerous and overcrowded," he said. Most shelters were designed to benefit society by hiding the problem rather than helping the homeless break cycles of poverty, dependency, and despair. A room full of cots was cost-effective but did little to help residents improve their situations (McDonald, 2016).

Lou was the fifth executive director in the first two years at the homeless center; nobody had lasted more than six months in the role. The center was $100,000 in debt and had eleven employees who were paid $5 an hour with no health benefits (McDonald, 2016).

Eventually, the place Lou envisioned – a comprehensive and integrated facility designed to break cycles rather than simply feed or house the homeless – took shape. After a few years, Lou and his team had set up a full-time Montessori preschool program, mental health counseling, a medical clinic, a drug and alcohol rehab center, adult education, job training programs, and a commercial landscape business that employed residents and former residents, all on the same campus (McDonald, 2016).

In eight years, Lou built the center into a regional and national powerhouse, establishing it as a model in addressing the complex issues involved in homelessness. The center became such a success that people visited from all over the country to learn from the model, and John Kasich, then a US congressman, invited Lou to speak to members of Congress (McDonald, 2016; University of Notre Dame, n.d.).

In all of this activity, raising money was last on Lou's mind until big dreams forced him to seek the necessary resources to build a sustainable model. In his quest to create an exemplary program, Lou exhibited formidable skills as a fundraiser – passionate about the need, compelling about the solutions his team was developing, and engaging with donors about how they could partner in the effort.

I was provost at Notre Dame in 2002 when then president, Father Edward Malloy, made the surprising appointment of Lou as vice president of university relations. The two had known each other since the days when Lou was a student, but it was a seismic jump from directing a local homeless shelter to overseeing philanthropy for a university of Notre Dame's stature and complexity (Moore, 2002).

Father Malloy took a bold step and bet on talent – a decision that many, including some trustees, questioned at the time. Lou inherited a good, if conventional, fundraising operation, which had completed a $1 billion campaign in 2000 and was poised for another significant fundraising effort. He led the "Spirit of Notre Dame" campaign, which raised more than $2 billion by 2011 (Brown, 2011; Moore, 2002).

What happened next is astonishing. In Notre Dame's subsequent campaign, which finished in 2020, the University raised over $5.3 billion, the largest campaign over a traditional seven-year span ever for an American university without a medical school (MacCready, 2020; Russell, 2022).

Lou executed that campaign with a powerful organization of some 325 staff. He attributes the success to two things: a clear and compelling vision and a relentless commitment to hiring staff of outstanding talent. On both fronts, Lou's perspective is highly unconventional.

Lou and his team convey the mission of Notre Dame with a burning intensity. Their theme sheds much of the elitism that surrounds top American universities. They are not advocating higher rankings, smarter students, more star faculty – although some of these advances are a means to a greater end. Their message is simple: How can Notre Dame become one of the most powerful means for good in the world? How can Notre Dame serve as a conduit to impact real world problems? Lou embodies that mission of service and makes doing good for the world the overarching theme of Notre Dame's identity – whether seeking hundreds of millions for new scholarships, enhancing biomedical research, designing more livable cities, or resolving conflicts in the most troubled areas of the world.

If one of Lou's passions is solving major human problems, the other is his almost obsessive concern for bringing talent to the team. I have never witnessed anyone who is more focused on recruiting and developing gifted leaders. When you speak with Lou about these matters, he begins by saying there are simply too many lazy searches: conventional job descriptions, standard hiring procedures, and predictable candidates – usually modest promotions for people who have worked in the same narrow field.

"Search consultants miss out on so much talent by typecasting candidates and staying within conventional lanes," he said recently. Reflecting his own highly unconventional journey, Lou looks for talent in places usual and unusual.

Lou began hiring above grade out of necessity at the homeless center. There, he sought out gifted young people to form a team, knowing he could pay them only $18,000 a year. He offered a four-part pitch: First, if you come to work for us, you will be hard pressed to find an organization with a clearer or deeper sense of mission. Second, we are asking you not only to execute your responsibilities at the highest level but also to be a cocreator in building a model worthy of replication throughout the country. Come and do what has never been done before. Third, as a pioneer in developing a more effective service model, you can have an impact on a national and even global scale. Fourth, you will be in the foxhole with a team that will challenge you to be your best every day and nurture you through difficult times. The work will be grueling, but you will be molded into a leader of tested strength and purpose. Seeking a few good men and women, Lou recruited a remarkable set of young leaders.

Now, as a senior leader, Lou continues to proclaim that his highest priority is recruiting the right people – people with differing strengths who can complement each other. With his organization always changing – last year hiring seventy new people – he challenges everyone on the team to scour for talent and add recruiting to their job descriptions. He evaluates leaders on their attention to that goal and keeps three active lists himself: (1) emerging talent within the university relations department, (2) emerging talent within the university, and (3) emerging talent in the broader world.

He invites his colleagues to think of every single hire as being of crucial importance – as if it were a marriage. We should complete a hire with the feeling of walking down the wedding aisle, pinching oneself in disbelief and awe. The threshold needs to be that we cannot believe anyone of this caliber is joining our team. Conversely, if we hire merely good people, we will be stuck with mediocrity for years to come. Less than stellar hiring is a sure sign that complacency is setting in. "A really good hire makes you reinvent yourself," Lou suggested.

Lou also has a distinct view of what to look for in a new hire. One must have appropriate skill sets and experience to do the job. That is a given. But he focuses on three other dimensions. First, is the candidate genuinely passionate about the mission? Passion is a multiplier force. Second, do they manifest integrity, character, and humility? One quality he searches for is whether candidates are ego-sturdy enough to put mission and others first. Nobody is inspired by a colleague looking out for themselves. And third, are they burning with hunger to achieve the great and the good? Lou adds that he will take hunger over expertise every day of the week.

Lou's passion and vision have driven Notre Dame's phenomenal success in philanthropy, but the real secret is the breadth and depth of talent he has enlisted. One striking measure of that quality is that, today, there are four vice presidents at Notre Dame who either came to the university or whose talents were nurtured over years in the development office.

Lou's appetite for talent has not only enhanced Notre Dame's fiscal stature but also strengthened Notre Dame's overall senior leadership team.

"If there's one thing to get right as a leader, it is surrounding yourself with talent that is better than yourself."

What I Learned

The first thing I have learned from watching Lou is his *relentless ambition for doing good*. Lou has an aversion to simply maintaining the current level of excellence. He sets the bar higher, dreams more boldly, and works hard to achieve those dreams. Before the last campaign was over, Lou began thinking about the next one: If the last campaign raised over $5 billion, what would it take to double that amount? He imagines it will take not only continuous improvement but also a paradigmatic shift in how they do business – and that, of course, will require innovation and continuing to infuse the organization with superb human talent.

A second lesson I have learned is that *mission, vision, and passion are all important*. What will inspire an organization to dream big and work hard? What will galvanize a community to move beyond self-interest and professional advancement? Is there a compelling mission that undergirds day-to-day work? In Notre Dame's case, what will motivate donors to stretch and give generously to an organization that is prosperous by anyone's measure? Lou's own paradoxical history – from shantytown and homeless center to working with super-wealthy donors – is a wonderful illustration of the power of the right kind of mission. It is one that is believed and lived.

I also learned from Lou to *strive always to hire above expected grade*. That is the principal way organizations will be renewed and move beyond the status quo. Lou has built an organization premised on this philosophy. Implementing this ideal requires tremendous effort and attention. It does not happen naturally. Each hire becomes the gene pool from which all activity flows. Convincing everyone in an organization to hire people better than themselves is always an uphill battle. However, it is one that Lou has proven can be successful.

Lou also taught me that *talent can come from varied quarters*. His own journey illustrates this, as does his success in finding leaders in one sector and moving them to another. His senior team has a regular process of evaluating the talents and prospects of everyone in the organization to ensure that gifts are best used and job responsibilities are repurposed, even if in unconventional ways.

Kevin White

5 Kevin White: Mentoring the Next Generation of Leaders

Kevin launches people.

Bernard Muir
Athletic Director, Stanford University

Kevin White is widely recognized as the unofficial dean of university athletic directors. Some refer to him as "the godfather" of intercollegiate sports. At latest count, Kevin has mentored thirty-one current athletic directors or other senior officials in collegiate athletics. He has been a perennial force – whether negotiating television rights for the then-PAC-10 Conference when he was at Arizona State University, representing Notre Dame to NBC, winning two national championships in men's basketball at Duke, or serving on the United States Olympic Committee.

I served on the search committee that recruited Kevin to Notre Dame as athletic director in 2000 (Notre Dame University, 2000). Coming to South Bend fulfilled a long-cherished dream of this Irish Catholic who grew up on Long Island. Kevin had a solid but not elite education, served as the assistant track and cross-country coach at Central Michigan University, and began working in athletic administration at Division III Loras College in Iowa (Duke University, n.d.). There was nothing in his early years – except for grit and hard work – to predict that this man would become such an influential figure in American collegiate athletics – at Notre Dame for eight years and then thirteen years at Duke University, where he recently retired (Duke University, n.d.).

From the time he stepped foot on the Notre Dame campus, Kevin was a whirlwind of activity – a connector. Before it was common, Kevin always had a cell phone in hand. He brought new expertise and operational excellence to the

Notre Dame athletic department. At both Notre Dame and Duke, Kevin regularly taught a much-sought-after business school course in sports management (Duke University, Fuqua School of Business, n.d.). Part of the attraction was the list of top sports executives that lectured week to week. Kevin knew everybody.

At Notre Dame, his initial and, I think, signature accomplishment was bringing fresh talent into the department. In the five years that we were there together, Kevin recruited Sandy Barbour, who went on to serve as the athletic director at University of California–Berkeley and then Penn State; Bernard Muir, who became AD at Stanford; and Jim Phillips, who became AD at Northwestern University and is now commissioner of the Atlantic Coast Conference. He also mentored Bubba Cunningham, now the AD at the University of North Carolina–Chapel Hill, and Bill Scholl, the AD at Marquette University. Working for him at Notre Dame and Duke was Boo Corrigan, now the AD at North Carolina State University; Stan Wilcox, who become the AD at Florida State and then executive vice president of regulatory affairs at the NCAA; and Nina King, who succeeded Kevin as AD at Duke.

Kevin linked his personal ambition to talent acquisition and development. He caught talented young people on their way up, invested in them, and facilitated their advancement in the profession. The distinct feature of the "White System" was that anyone coming to work for Kevin understood that the job was not permanent: Kevin would work with them for a few years and then help them leave the nest – learning to fly for themselves at another institution. Kevin's philosophy was that it was better to have great and emerging talent for a few years than not at all.

White's approach resembles what Sydney Finkelstein found among those talented leaders he calls "superbosses." These leaders, like Bill Walsh in football or Julian Robertson in investing, had the gift of mentoring "trees of talent," inspiring young leaders and launching their careers (Finkelstein, 2016).

"The first time that we met when I was an assistant AD, he sat down with me and asked me what was important to me – what I wanted to do professionally," Cunningham shared. "Not only did he really listen and take it to heart, he was exceptionally helpful and guided me in the direction to set me up for success."

Kevin looked for young talent with real ambition. "This relationship will not work unless you're pretty aspirational," he told them. He wanted staff who were hungry, and one of his key criteria for hiring was the demonstrated passion and intensity that one brought to their work.

I once asked Kevin how this informal system came to be. He said it evolved out of sheer necessity. In his early positions, at Loras College and the University of Maine, resources were so scarce that it seemed impossible to build competitive programs. Kevin's answer was to give opportunity to talented, hungry young people.

Kevin recruited young people by discussing two kinds of compensation – direct and indirect. The former would be minimal, but the great promise was in the latter. The indirect compensation was what Kevin and his team could do to build their career. "So, throw in with us," Kevin would say. "Trust us, and at some point, you will go to that indirect career window, and you'll get your payout … If you really want to move up the food chain, we can help you."

The promise of Kevin's indirect window was a threefold kind of leadership development. First, one would become part of a strong team and learn week to week about all facets of athletic administration.

"He created an environment where everybody can learn from each other," said Muir. "I learned so much from my peers and whom I was surrounded by when I worked with Kevin, and that allowed me to aspire to be an AD."

Second, Kevin promised cross-training, experience in the full range of activities within an athletic department: in compliance, event management, fundraising, academics, and administration of individual sports. The long view – becoming a senior athletic director – would be always kept in mind.

"For thirteen years, we were together at Duke," said King, "and he was intentional about including me in decision making, in understanding every facet of the department, in vision strategy – all of it. I didn't realize it, but he was preparing me the whole time we were together. He always took me with him – even when I wasn't invited. Nobody ever questioned when Kevin walked into the room with a plus one – even though there may not have been an invitation. No one ever questioned it."

A third and vitally important commitment was not to violate the integrity of the system. That meant refusing to hire senior staff that would block a person's advance – in Kevin's words, "cutting the line." Undergirding all of this was Kevin's demonstrated interest in the individual and their own development. Over time, young people saw Kevin deliver on behalf of his people, again and again.

Both Jim Phillips, the commissioner of the Atlantic Coast Conference, and Nina King, Duke's current athletic director, attest to Kevin's deep commitment to his staff. In a real sense, they became family. Phillips, who worked for Kevin at both Arizona State and Notre Dame, said that it was the first time he had a real role model and mentor, other than his own father. King, who began working for Kevin as a student intern at Notre Dame, says she was treated like a family member from day one. "He does mentorship the best," King concluded. "There is simply no one better … He really knows how to help people succeed in this business."

Both also give great credit to Kevin's wife, Jane, whose commitment to Kevin's young staff members always seemed as strong as his own. Their joint approach to young staff, while deeply professional, was also deeply personal. "It was like we were mentored at the kitchen table," King observed.

Kevin suggested that this kind of deep loyalty was essential: "Who is going to follow somebody and do something they wouldn't ordinarily do without this person being involved in their personal and professional life?"

Over his forty-year career, Kevin has always been an effective champion of diversity. I observed him effectively recruit, mentor, and advance women and persons of color at both Notre Dame and at Duke. For the last decade at Duke, he and King established a special internship program that included as many as ten recent graduates from around the country interested in careers in athletic adminis-tration. A number of talented next-generation leaders have come out of that program.

When Kevin retired from collegiate athletics, he left his fingerprints on nearly all facets of the industry.

What I Learned

Kevin illustrated that *change was constant and adaptability essential for effective leadership*. Bernard Muir said that Kevin regularly counseled his staff: "Put up the periscope." Understand the changes all around and adapt accordingly. One lesson Kevin learned from serving at several universities and watching his associates take on positions at many others was that there were no cookie-cutter solutions. Each situation and set of challenges called for solutions particular to that time and place.

Kevin was a *model mentor*, and I learned from him what that required. He could see the promise in a young person and push them with a deft hand to build their leadership portfolio. His interest was genuine and deeply personal. Between him and Jane, it was downright familial.

For all his business savvy and investment in leadership development, Kevin *never lost focus on students, their welfare, and development*. He attended every athletic event that was humanly possible. I recall him flying all the way to California one day to watch a collegiate tennis match and then back the next night on a red-eye flight. Kevin's infectious love for college athletics stemmed from his genuine love of student athletes.

Finally, Kevin was a person of *unflinching integrity and loyalty*. When he took a position out of conviction, there was no further discussion, and on those issues, he could sometimes appear stubborn. He was intensely competitive and his whole visage would change when his team was losing. Literally, he would turn ashen gray. For him, the enterprise of college athletics was much more than winning and losing; it was about doing what he deemed was right. That involved deep loyalty to the student athletes for whom he was responsible, the administrators to whom he reported, and the coaches and staff with whom he worked. I might disagree with Kevin White, but I never once doubted that I could trust him.

Jill Tiefenthaler

6 Jill Tiefenthaler: Letting Leaders Lead

One thing that I saw in Jill was joyous courage ... pushing us to do what we didn't think we could do.

Emily Chan
Dean of the Faculty, Colorado College

A year after I arrived at Wake Forest, we began searching for its next provost – the chief academic officer. This was a critical appointment because academic life at Wake Forest, many thought, was languishing. Faculty morale was poor and compensation seriously below market. Going to faculty meetings was no pleasure. As the new president, I was regularly peppered with questions about inadequate compensation. There were few fresh academic initiatives and most faculty believed that the chief financial officer, rather than the provost, was determining university academic priorities.

A new provost needed to restore the trust of the faculty, launch a strategic plan, and restore academic priorities to the center of university life. In my mind, the stakes were high and required fresh energy.

As part of our national search, I called Judith McLaughlin, the director of the Harvard Seminar for New Presidents, which I had attended the previous summer. Her networks were broad and deep across higher education. Judy made several suggestions, among them someone she described as a long shot. She had heard of a very dynamic, young economist at Colgate University named Jill Tiefenthaler. Jill had been recently promoted to full professor, chaired the economics department, and was working with President Rebecca Chopp on strategic issues and trustee matters (National Geographic Society, n.d.).

In this way, Jill became part of our search. Among several great candidates, Jill clearly stood out. Despite her limited credentials, the search committee was taken by her knowledge of higher education, strategic outlook, and infectious joy about the whole process of teaching and learning. In even brief conversation with Jill, one saw key elements of transformative leadership: self-confidence, institutional ambition, an engaging style, and a great sense of humor. The committee also noted that she was an attentive listener.

With a unanimous vote of the search committee, I offered Jill the position and worked hard to recruit her to Wake Forest – along with her husband, Kevin Rask, also an economist, and their two young children. We were aided in the process because Jill and Kevin both had earned their doctoral degrees at Duke University and were familiar with North Carolina.

We took nothing for granted, rolling out the red carpet in every way possible. A Wake Forest trustee kindly lent his jet to whisk Jill and Kevin from upstate New York to Winston-Salem. At forty-two, and with only modest administrative experience, Jill became the youngest – and first woman – provost in the history of Wake Forest.

Later, when asked about her decision to come to Wake Forest, Jill recalled she was convinced that she would be "surrounded by high-quality people who had big ambitions and wanted to do transformative things." What was decisive for her was a sense that "this was a special time for Wake Forest," and that "I was going to have support and a lot of autonomy. Nathan didn't recruit you and then put his thumb on you."

Jill generated creative change in her four years at Wake Forest. There is a line from Shakespeare that comes to mind about many academics I have known: "Good talkers are no good doers" (Shakespeare, 2001). That was certainly not the case with Jill. From day one, Jill was a great doer. She relished big and challenging tasks, such as taking the lead in crafting the university's next strategic plan. The university had begun strategic planning the spring before she arrived, and she would later laugh that, when she first stepped into her Wake Forest office, there were seventy-five plans from distinct departments and programs on her desk.

Jill assembled a talented team of associate provosts, including several of the university's most respected faculty members, and together, in a remarkably short time – often working nights and weekends – crafted the outline of a compelling strategic plan.

The heart of that plan was a positive assertion of Wake Forest's distinct identity as a "collegiate university." In the past, Wake Forest had suffered from negative connotations of *not* being a liberal arts college and *not* being a research-intensive university. What the strategic plan clarified, and Jill put into practice, was the celebration of the distinct niche of teaching like a college – with redoubled efforts in faculty–student engagement – and enjoyment of the benefits of a university – law, medicine, business, divinity, and big-time sports (Wake Forest University, n.d.).

The strategic plan was bold in being both radically traditional and radically innovative. Unlike many emerging universities that clamored to line up as the next research powerhouse, Wake Forest chose to underscore its role in teaching and mentoring. Wake Forest would seek the very best and brightest teacher-scholars – not the reverse. The plan also underscored Wake Forest's traditional distinctive of attempting to educate the whole person.

At the same time, the plan espoused many fresh initiatives. Faculty were invited to develop new interdisciplinary initiatives, and great efforts were made to provide new financial aid and diversify the campus. Under Jill's direction, the university began its first women's center and its first LGBTQ center. The office of campus ministry created positions for a Jewish chaplain and a Muslim chaplain. Major investment was made to enhance opportunity for first generation students; the Magnolia Scholars Program provided highly effective mentoring and guidance to that end.

The most daring initiative that Jill proposed – in collaboration with Martha Allman, the dean of admissions at the time – was for Wake Forest to implement test-optional admissions. Starting with the class entering in 2009, Wake Forest became the first top-30 national university to forgo requiring SAT or ACT scores for college admissions. Jill's own expertise as an economist of higher education gave us all confidence that this was the right decision – and one that, over the last decade and as a result of the pandemic, has spread widely in American higher education.

Jill and I were great partners in taking on challenging initiatives. We implemented a plan to combine graduate and undergraduate business schools into one – when the faculty of both opposed. In order to address the critical issue of faculty salaries and provide greater support for financial aid, we developed a plan to increase the student body by 500 students over five years. That plan worked marvelously – with no loss of student quality – and allowed us to substantially enhance faculty salaries at the very moment of the economic downturn of 2008–9.

Jill loved to tackle fresh challenges. When the information technology functions at Wake Forest seemed to be floundering, Jill gladly took them under her wing. When the student affairs division needed fresh energy, Jill convinced me to have that group report to her; thereafter, there was no shortage of ideas and programs to enliven the student experience.

Jill left a remarkable legacy at Wake Forest before becoming president of Colorado College, where, in nine years, she demonstrated the same kind of transformative leadership on a broader scale. There, she earned the loving nickname from students of "Chief Tief." Jill spent a year of intensive listening to the community, then championed a dramatic strategic plan that strengthened the college's distinct tradition of "block" teaching and set an ambitious plan for the future. She excelled at bringing the campus together around aspirational plans (Hanna, 2020).

One great example was the fate of the campus library, long a source of complaint. Designed in 1962, the original Tutt Library bore all the hallmarks of the then-dominant contemporary academic architectural style: brutalist and introverted, an enigmatic concrete box. Without the option of demolition, Jill brought people together to ask what could be done. The result was an expanded and transformed library, "wrapping" the original building with extensive glass with sweeping views of the Colorado range and adding cutting-edge teaching and collaborative space (*The Colorado Springs Business Journal*, 2014).

Jill was also a very personal and authentic mentor to young leaders. The current dean of the faculty at Colorado College, Emily Chan, explains how Jill sought her out when she was a new associate dean and asked, "What can I do to support you?" In a set of ongoing conversations, Jill shared her own experience about professional and family life. "She saw me as a whole person and shared her whole person. ... When we talked about career, she actually talked about family." Jill also encouraged other senior administrators to visit with Emily and began to expand her contacts.

At both Wake Forest and Colorado College, Jill had an infectious way of changing the collective imagination. She asked why not rather than why; is there a better way to handle a problem, tackle an issue, or address a concern? She had an amazing capacity to learn new things quickly and suggest alternate approaches and solutions. That spirit is an amazing gift in any organization, but particularly so in higher education with its tendency to stick to well-worn paths.

Early in 2020, Jill was named CEO of the National Geographic Society, one of the largest nonprofit educational and scientific organizations in the world (National Geographic Society, 2020). She continues to demonstrate her keen eye, leadership, and creativity there.

What I Learned

Jill taught me that it is *great to have a colleague with different values and priorities to complement your own gifts.* She was passionate about making Wake Forest more diverse and developing interdisciplinary programs. I was more focused on institutional realignment – particularly in business and medicine – and on issues of vocation and character. Today, Wake Forest is a much stronger place because the institution moved on these complementary fronts.

Jill encouraged me to *experiment and take risks, knowing that every venture would not be successful.* Our experiment in implementing a test-optional admission process was a striking success. Other initiatives, like funding new interdisciplinary centers, were less so. But the dynamic tone that Jill brought to the provost's office encouraged other leaders around the university to become more venturesome. One will never develop an innovative organization if the standard is that every new venture must succeed.

I also learned from Jill that one must *resist the impulse to control.* In the diffuse power structure of higher education, trying to exercise too much control is as great a danger as not exercising enough. One needs to focus on what is really important and strategic, freeing other leaders to use their creativity to make decisions and address issues. Jill once said that micromanagers are killers of talent. Jill and I rarely disagreed on overall direction and strategy, but both of us knew that she needed plenty of elbow room to exercise her creativity and vision. I happily granted that given what she accomplished and the strength she brought to the overall organization.

Jill is a transformative leader who did not back away from thorny issues and was very nimble in finding creative solutions. She worked tirelessly, inspired creativity, held high aspirations, and exercised flexibility in order to achieve ambitious dreams.

Steve Reinemund

7 Steve Reinemund: Linking Performance and Character

He had a style about himself that I have never seen before in any other CEO. He could be tough as nails without scaring you to death, but he could also be as gentle as he needed to be in any situation.

David Dupree
Trustee, Wake Forest University

One of the great thrills of my professional life was an unexpected phone call I received early in 2008 from Steve Reinemund. Steve had been CEO of PepsiCo and was one of the most respected business leaders in America and the world (Fyten, 2008; Halpern, n.d.). In watching Steve chair the National Advisory Committee for the Salvation Army ("Steven Reinemund," 2023), I caught a glimpse of his magnetism and generosity as a leader.

Early in my tenure at Wake Forest, I invited Steve to speak at a summer retreat for trustees and participate in a national conference at Wake Forest that took an in-depth look at the issues of vocation across a wide range of professions.

But the call that day came unannounced. Steve prefaced the conversation by asking me to listen and keep from giving any immediate response. I agreed. At the time, we were well along in a search for a new dean of business at Wake Forest and, as it turned out, that was the subject of Steve's call.

Steve asked if Wake Forest would ever consider a nontraditional candidate for the dean's position. From afar, he had become intrigued thinking about the position. As I had promised, I did not offer an immediate reaction, but my mind began to race as I imagined the possibilities of a leader of this stature coming to Wake Forest to reimagine management education.

Jill Tiefenthaler, then-provost, and I immediately began to engage Steve about the challenges and opportunities at Wake Forest. Don Flow, a Wake Forest trustee who also knew Steve, was crucial in describing the impact Steve could make and the community the Reinemunds could enjoy at Wake Forest.

Within a couple weeks, Steve called to say that he and his wife, Gail, were inclined to accept the appointment, but there was one additional hurdle. For the Reinemunds to move from Dallas – with two teenage children still at home – the entire family had to come to a consensus that the move was right. After a family visit to Winston-Salem, we waited several weeks for the Reinemunds to make their decision. When the family voted, it was unanimous.

I have often thought how amazing it was that Steve chose to come to Wake Forest, a school whose MBA program was not in the top 25 and was struggling to align two undersized and underfunded business schools – graduate and undergraduate.

Steve, it seemed, had never done anything in his life that wasn't the best of the best. He turned down Ivy Leagues to attend the Naval Academy (Fyten, 2008). As a Marine officer, he served at the White House where he became the Presenting Officer, introducing distinguished guests at receptions for President Gerald and First Lady Betty Ford (Halpern, n.d.; "Steven Reinemund," 2023). After Steve completed his MBA, Marriott CEO Bill Marriott recruited him for a fast-track leadership development program ("Steven Reinemund," 2023). By the age of thirty-eight, Steve was CEO of Pizza Hut and launched its first initiative into home delivery. He then became CEO of Frito-Lay, and under his leadership, sales and profits rose steadily between 1993 and 1999. In 1999, Steve was named president and COO of PepsiCo, and in 2001, he was appointed chairman and CEO. During his five-year tenure in the top post, PepsiCo's revenues increased by more than $9 billion and the company's market capitalization rose above $100 billion – surpassing above Coca-Cola for the first time (Fyten, 2008). His organizations' performances and his individual accolades are many and varied, but in addition to business success, Steve was widely known for his ability to relate to and understand his employees (Halpern, n.d.).

Why, then, did Steve choose to come to Wake Forest? The first reason was his deep commitment to give back and help students find their purpose. Steve sought to bring vocational discernment and character development into the core of management programs. As a serious person of faith, Steve looked for opportunities to invest in young people.

Second, there was a clear alignment of vision. I was deeply interested in Wake Forest focusing on issues of character – on educating the whole person. On these matters, Steve and I shared a common interest; he knew he would have conversation partners and institutional support for initiatives in the business school. Steve's leadership had always been values-driven, and Wake Forest gave him the opportunity to bring that approach into the heart of management education.

Third, Steve also knew that Wake Forest would be open to innovation and rethinking programs and curricula. He once confessed to me that he found Wake Forest more interesting a challenge than the business schools at Harvard or Stanford, because it was a school on the move and could be nimbler and more flexible in its approach – with no vaunted reputation to defend.

With his commanding presence, engaging smile, and track record of performance, Steve became dean of business at Wake Forest in 2008 (Wake Forest University School of Business, 2008). From day one, he faced a daunting challenge: the integration of two separate business schools. The Calloway School of Business and Accountancy and the Babcock Graduate School of Management had separate buildings, and their respective faculty did not want to be together (Fyten, 2008).

Under those conditions, Steve began to work his magic. He listened intently to his colleagues and learned about the fears and the aspirations of the faculty. He asked the search committee to become his ongoing advisory committee. And, most importantly, he began to articulate a compelling vision for the school that promised to enhance the reputation and academic life of everyone. Steve demonstrated his remarkable ability to have a stated goal in mind and to execute in a way that was convincing. Within three months of becoming dean, the faculties of both schools, with virtual unanimity, voted to become one (Fyten, 2008).

These early days demonstrated Steve's rare leadership qualities, especially embodying qualities that often do not go together. He was forceful, even intimidating, and a great listener. He was driven and caring, competitive, and empathetic. "He was a giant in terms of his reputation and execution but also a great friend," one colleague noted. He was absolutely committed to results and insisted on always doing things the right way. He was highly disciplined and amazingly flexible in adjusting to the new environment of higher education. He was a master strategist and renowned for executing details.

Above all, Steve was committed to students. He never turned down student requests for counsel and spent endless hours exploring professional opportunities for them. He was serious when he set an institutional goal of 100 percent placement for graduate and undergraduate students. Early in his tenure, he invited students to join him at 6:30 a.m. on Thursdays for "Dawn with the Dean" – a three-mile run. On a typical Thursday, more than 100 students would take this opportunity to rub shoulders with the dean, ask him questions, and share whatever was on their minds (Wake Forest University School of Business, 2013).

Steve was a master strategist and visionary who rethought the business programs. At a time when there was waning interest in the MBA, Steve championed a new one-year master's in management for liberal arts students (Wake Forest University School of Business, n.d.). This program, adopted by many other schools, had an intense focus on diversity. Steve enlisted major scholarship support from a wide range of national companies to ensure the program would serve diverse and underrepresented populations. Within a couple of years, this master's degree became the most diverse program at Wake Forest, with about 40 percent of students from underrepresented backgrounds. The connection with companies also ensured that students had ready access to positions upon graduation (Wake Forest University School of Business, n.d.).

Steve also had a creative vision about building a new home for the integrated School of Business. As planning began, he established a core group of donors who became great friends and fervent supporters of Steve's vision. On my shelf, I have a napkin sketch – now in Lucite – from a meeting with that group that represents the core idea for the building. In the middle is a "living room" – a central place for interchange and study for students and faculty – with offices, classrooms, study, and administrative space radiating out from it. Ultimately, Steve's vision was to bring people together in active conversation through space (Anderson, 2013; Henson, 2011).

In this planning process, Steve became friends with Wake Forest parents Mike and Mary Farrell, who were quickly captured by Steve's vision and what they saw at Wake Forest. In Mike's words, "We went there looking for academics, and we found a place where there was a discussion about community service, faith *and* academics" (Henson, 2011). In 2008, at the height of the financial crisis, the Farrells made the bold commitment of $10 million as the lead gift for this new facility. Today, almost anyone at Wake Forest would say that Farrell Hall stands as the most beautiful and inviting building on the campus. Day or night, one sees scores of students studying or in conversation – the realization of Steve's dream of a place of welcome and interaction. (Anderson, 2011; Henson, 2011).

Steve also lifted the stature of the School of Business in corporate America. He brought CEOs of major corporations to campus and convinced them to recruit Wake Forest students; he upgraded the quality of executives on the school's advisory council; and he pushed the school to design programs with an "unrivaled connection to the market."

Steve was also shrewd in discerning what he could do best and what others around him could do better. He did not have the patience to engage in prolonged faculty discussion and debate – so he left that to others. He focused on high-level strategy, clarifying the core mission and identity of the school, and expanding contacts and opportunities in the corporate world. On those matters, he was brilliant and transformative.

What I Learned

The first thing I learned from Steve was to *have focused goals*. He has a great gift of sorting through complexity and discerning what is most important. He was a master at deciding what two or three goals would make the most difference. On these few matters, he focused with laser-like intensity. He conveyed to all constituents exactly what the goals were. There was clarity and transparency, which built a great deal of trust.

Steve showed that *leaders can be demanding and caring*. Being achievement-oriented and people-oriented are not mutually exclusive. Steve understood people and cared for them; that never diminished his drive for excellence. He was engaging, winsome, and understood where people were coming from; that did not limit his very high expectations for individuals and for the organization. In my judgment, his greatest single gift was holding both commitments in creative tension.

A disciplined person, Steve believed that *character is formed by ingrained, steady habits*. He demanded of himself and others day-to-day accountability, believing that organizational improvement came by regular and sustained execution. When he spoke of finding a job for every graduate, he did not mean grand rhetoric around some lofty plan. He meant working intensely with each individual student and trying to match them – with all their strengths and weaknesses – with an appropriate employer.

Steve brought excellence to every dimension of his professional life, by his demeanor, by his treatment of faculty and staff, by the distinguished guests that were regular visitors to campus, and by his clear and inspiring vision. In that way, he helped everyone think differently about management education at Wake Forest.

Andy Chan

8 Andy Chan: Unleashing Personal and Career Development

Andy is a visionary and inspirational person and leader … The tremendous program Andy has developed at Wake Forest University is transforming how our future leaders will lead.

Sheila Madden
Executive Coach

From the time Steve Reinemund introduced me to Andy Chan, I was intrigued by his approach to career development. At the time, Andy led the career services office at Stanford Business School and mentored Steve's son, Jonathan, an MBA student. What I found fascinating is that Andy's approach to students pushed them to think about careers in more profound ways than merely seeking a well-paying job. At Stanford, he taught a seminar, "Career and Life Vision," and asked students to reflect on their purpose, core values, life experience, and aspirations, and how those should shape their professional choices (Duke Divinity, 2013). He used the platform of career services – a most conventional function – to ask fundamental philosophical and vocational questions. Who am I, really, and how should that affect my professional choices (Duke Divinity, 2013)?

Andy's approach aligned very much with my own thinking about the importance of vocational discernment. In 2009, after meeting with Andy at Stanford, I asked if he would visit Wake Forest and evaluate our career services program. We were seeking a new director of that effort, and it was logical to stop and take stock. A few weeks after Andy offered his assessment, we invited him back for a weeklong consultation to evaluate our whole approach to career services in both the liberal arts and the business school.

On that visit, a cross-university, multidisciplinary team of faculty, students, and administrators brainstormed about what could be done if one imagined moving career services from the periphery to the center of the college experience. Andy was intrigued with this vision, and those discussions led to an invitation for him to come to Wake Forest as the inaugural vice president of personal and career development on the president's cabinet – the first such position in American higher education (Dominus, 2013).

Andy entered Wake Forest with a powerful vision, particularly in a time when the value of a liberal arts education was under assault and faculty in some departments were witnessing fewer student majors. "Unless we can demonstrate to prospective students and their families that the four years spent at college will result in better employment prospects, there will continue to be those who disparage a college education as a waste of money," Andy wrote in a seminal white paper highlighting strategic change with career development at colleges across the country, "Transforming the College-to-Career Experience" (Chan & Derry, 2013).

Consequently, the stated goal of Andy's vision, the Office of Personal and Career Development (OPCD), was simple: "to provide every Wake Forest student with the tools and confidence to navigate the uncertain, unpredictable path from college to career." The invitation to students was bold and straightforward: "We seek to inspire, support, and prepare you to find opportunities that reflect your interests and values and create a foundation for a meaningful life" (Wake Forest University, n.d.). The goal was job placement, to be sure, but much more.

In creating something new, Andy faced enormous challenges. Faculty and staff had certain conventional notions about career services, which I once described as placing that office "somewhere just below parking" as a matter of administrative priority (Dominus, 2013). Early on, I asked him where Wake Forest stood comparatively in career services, and he answered, "About 3 out of 10." Not very good. The office had been far too inwardly focused and did not have strong external connections with all types of organizations nationwide, from government to nonprofit to technology, finance organizations, and consulting firms. In addition, Wake Forest had followed a conventional pattern of separate career offices for liberal arts and business students.

From day one, Andy was a big thinker and strategic campus politician who excelled in building bridges. He spent months meeting and listening to faculty, staff, and students across the university, assessing potential partners interested in renewing efforts in personal and career development. One of the most important partnerships was with the business school and its dean, Steve Reinemund.

They agreed that the best strategy was for Wake Forest to have one career services operation, which would greatly enhance Wake Forest's position with potential employers – a major priority – and upgrade the numerous, wide-ranging internship and job opportunities for liberal arts students. When premier employers came to campus, they could interview the very best Wake Forest students – whatever their field of study.

After a year, Andy reimagined the profile of the OPCD and remodeled a large suite of offices, which were open and cutting-edge, creating a welcoming, relaxed, and contemporary atmosphere for student engagement. He also convinced the university to introduce the OPCD to parents and students from the very beginning – during first-year orientation weekend. His approach attracted the attention of the *New York Times Magazine*, and in 2013, Susan Dominus wrote a breakthrough feature article, "How to Get a Job with a Philosophy Degree," which outlined Andy's introductory session with new students (Dominus, 2013).

Andy readily acknowledged the tension inherent between a liberal arts education and a focus on professional development. Believing that "a liberal arts education is the key to navigating change," Andy advised parents to allow students to explore areas of study – philosophy, anthropology, art – that might seem impractical on the surface. "Your child can be academically happy and still end up professionally successful," he told them (Dominus, 2013). Andy believed that studying what you love and professional development were entirely complementary; giving creative attention to the latter actually freed students to pursue the liberal arts.

Under Andy's leadership, Wake Forest has become the national model for creating a college-to-career community designed to prepare students to lead lives that matter, not just secure a first job after graduation (Wake Forest University, n.d.). He quickly became a catalyst for transforming the entire industry of career services. In the spring of 2012, Wake Forest hosted a national conference, "Rethinking Success: From the Liberal Arts to Careers in the 21st Century," with sessions that explored the innovative ways of rethinking the connections between the liberal arts and the world of work (Chan & Derry, 2013). The following year, in 2013, Andy gave a TEDx talk titled "Career Services Must Die" (TEDx Talks, 2013). It sent shock waves across the profession of career services. Andy was frank as to why most students – as well as parents, alumni, and even employers – are annoyed, even angry, about what they find in career offices. Then, he described the fresh and intensive model that was being implemented at Wake Forest that more adequately addressed the dynamics of today's world and students' needs.

Andy's contributions came to extend across the university. As a cabinet member, he brought fresh eyes, probing questions, and keen insight to a wide range of issues. Drawing upon his early experience as a consultant and his deep experience in Silicon Valley and with leading venture-backed startups, Andy pushed Wake Forest to innovate in its quest to become a distinct "collegiate university."

Recognizing Andy's role as a catalyst for innovation, Wake Forest made the decision to expand his responsibilities – naming him vice president of innovation and career services. In his expanded role, Andy coordinated a major two-year initiative to rethink priorities, develop new sources of income, and streamline expenses. Serving as an internal consultant, Andy led Wake Forest's administration and trustees through a process that re-examined bedrock assumptions and orthodoxies of the university. The comprehensive, design thinking-oriented process led to increased undergraduate enrollment by 500 students; launched new academic initiatives to link undergraduate education to the biomedical sciences; expanded a downtown research park; and created an engineering program for undergraduates in conjunction with the medical school, as well as many other exciting experiments and initiatives. The university also launched its first new school in two decades – the School for Professional Studies located in Charlotte (Wake Forest University, 2022).

Andy's leadership style was complex, combining an intense drive to accomplish with a deep interest in people. He was not always the easiest person to work for. "If you are going to be on Andy's team," long-term colleague Mercy Eyadiel noted, "you're going to have to hustle. You're going to have to do your homework. You're going to have to be prepared. And that's not always something people are prepared to do."

Andy asked his employees probing questions about how they thought about their decisions – pushing them to be more thoughtful and reflective about their actions. At the same time, he was not a micromanager. He established a vision and set high standards, but he expected leaders to chart their own path to achieve those goals.

And he had a gift for developing leaders. Several of his colleagues went on to lead career services offices at other universities. Across the higher education industry, Andy has mentored and advised many colleagues who are transforming career services at their respective institutions. Other longtime employees flourished in distinct niches that amplified their gifts.

At Wake Forest, Andy established a vastly different model of career services and became a catalyst for rethinking college-to-career preparation across the country. At the same time, he became a major force for innovation and strategic thinking within the university.

What I Learned

Andy widened my horizons by teaching me *the value of being a multilingual leader*. He could converse actively with students, faculty and staff, donors, parents, venture capitalists, and a wide range of business leaders. This ability grew out of his innate curiosity, keen interest in people, and ability to pay attention and listen. Andy never tried to dominate meetings but led with questions showing a genuine interest in what others were thinking and doing.

After listening to others, Andy *unselfishly offers advice and counsel* for people far and wide. At the top of the list were students whom he continued to advise and mentor even as alumni. Andy's instincts were never to hold good ideas to himself. Instead, he readily listened and counseled as many people and institutions as possible – including hundreds of colleges and universities that sought his wisdom about career services.

On the president's cabinet, Andy taught me *the value of having a devil's advocate*. He was not afraid to question assumptions and conclusions that most thought were self-evident. At first, some found it annoying, but over time, it had a leavening effect, freeing others to raise questions and consider alternate perspectives. The cabinet became far more adept at addressing difficult issues and disagreeing with each other in a context of trust.

Andy believes strongly that *most people are uniquely good at something, and one must seek what that is*. He admits that, in his own case, he did not find that until he was around forty years old, when he began working in higher education and started assisting students in thinking about their professional futures. He was good at many things, but his passion was helping others understand themselves better and translating that to a life of work. Andy's great gift has been helping people find and navigate a challenging path of vocational discernment in a deeply personal and holistic way.

Michele Gillespie

9 Michele Gillespie: Living Out Institutional Values

Michele is trustworthy and has a long track record of standing by her word and operating out of good intentions.

Rick Matthews
Professor of Physics, Wake Forest University

Michele Gillespie represents a strikingly different form of leadership from Andy Chan. Andy came into Wake Forest from outside and built something from scratch that hadn't existed before. Michele, by contrast, was an insider who had been deeply nourished by the culture of Wake Forest, coming into her own as teacher and scholar in Wake Forest's history department. Her path to leadership shows the great value of internal development.

Michele was a young history professor on the search committee that selected me to come to Wake Forest in 2005. From the start, I thought she represented the heart and soul of the university. A beloved teacher, an emerging star in the field of Southern United States history (Wake Forest University, n.d.), and a consummate colleague, Michele personified what Wake Forest aspired to be.

During my first year at Wake Forest, I consulted with Michele on a number of occasions as I sought to fathom the culture of the place. Her counsel was always thoughtful and wise. When I launched a search for a new provost, I asked Michele to join the search committee. That allowed her to get to know Jill Tiefenthaler even before Jill assumed her responsibilities as provost.

Michele had not aspired to move into administration, and she was surprised when Jill asked her to join her team. In her role as associate provost for academic initiatives, Michele brought infectious energy and curiosity. She was a major force in crafting a university strategic plan. She managed a diverse portfolio, including a university press, a public radio station, and a range of grant-funded centers. Michele's introduction to administration was positive in every way. She loved the work and found the provost's team exhilarating – even fun.

After three years in the provost's office, Michele stepped away and returned to her first calling to teach and write history. She had greater goals for herself as an historian; she knew she had another big book to write. "I knew, in my heart of hearts, that I would never be happy with myself . . . until I finished that book," she said.

After five years tilling the historical vineyard, with considerable accomplishments as scholar and teacher, Michele accepted the university's invitation to become dean of Wake Forest College and its twenty-nine departments, sixteen interdisciplinary programs, and more than 480 faculty (Wake Forest University, n.d.). For seven years, from 2015 to 2022, Michele took on this challenge with great energy and enthusiasm.

Some thought that Michele's gracious manner and deep connections within the college might thwart efforts for change and real advance. But what Michele displayed was a firmness couched with outward gentleness – an iron fist in a velvet glove. She reveled in the opportunity to lift Wake Forest to the same level of excellence that she had set for herself.

This trait was cultivated in Michele's approach to teaching history. On the one hand, she brought a noncontroversial style and deep respect for Southern history into the classroom. On the other, she tackled controversial issues – how race, class, gender, and sexuality affect history. "I challenge assumptions and take on Southern heroes," she once confessed. "It's good to challenge assumptions; intellectual discomfort is a good thing."

Michele applied the same kind of gracious determination to her job as dean. For example, she launched a process to reexamine general education requirements, something that Wake Forest had not done for over two decades. General education curriculum reviews are fraught with controversy and hazard, and Wake Forest was no exception. Yet Michele did not back away from the challenge. She set up a two-year process for faculty to undertake a complete assessment of general education requirements.

That process was long and tortuous; it included thirty-one committee meetings, two full-day retreats, twenty-nine meetings with departments and programs, and seven faculty forums. Some faculty complained about the process itself; others pushed one theme or another; and others resisted any change that would diminish their own department's role. Near the conclusion of the process, one group of faculty attempted to scuttle the whole effort with demands that the curriculum focus on racism and white supremacy, while another pushed against an interdisciplinary ethical inquiry requirement.

Through it all, Michele stayed the course, built coalitions, remained calm in the face of attack, and made mid-course corrections. Come what may, she remained resolute to achieve the larger aim of the faculty approving a new curriculum. That goal was tenaciously achieved – despite faculty division and in the face of the COVID pandemic with faculty meetings and votes taking place on Zoom.

Michele's deanship included many other notable achievements: the launching of an undergraduate engineering program (Neal, 2017) and a new downtown research campus (Walker, 2017); the creation of a new environmental studies major (Wake Forest University, n.d.) and an inaugural African-American Studies Program; and the shepherding of a new, robust program in leadership and character (Wake Forest University, n.d.). She brought refreshing energy and vision to the college's external board of visitors. She also guided the college through the complicated season of the pandemic.

Michele met these and many other challenges because of several vital dimensions of her leadership. First, she is a person of absolute integrity. Her actions, day after day, proved that she could be trusted; she was not operating with ulterior motives. "She went into administration because she thought she could make a difference for the university," Rick Matthews noted. "I never saw anything, on any occasion, where she would choose what was better for her professionally over what was better for the university."

Michele also prized relationships. She took people seriously and thought the best of them. She listened and engaged, never showing pique or a vindictive streak – even when people seemed unreasonable or self-serving. She stayed true to her principles, and she trusted people. This, in turn, generated a level of trust even when controversial decisions had to be made. Few faculty would ever say that Michele did not treat them fairly.

In keeping with her own convictions, Michele faced conflictive situations by returning to the stated mission of the college, which called for teacher-scholars to be invested deeply in their research and the lives of their students. She believed it, lived it, and held it as the standard by which all faculty and departments should operate. On this basis, she sought common ground.

Her infectious optimism also energized the organization. "Whenever I left a meeting with her, I felt empowered and encouraged," colleague Rebecca Alexander noted. Even in the worst days of the pandemic or during a crisis, Michele approached the issue with a calm determination: We will get through this. "She's unfailingly positive even in the face of daunting circumstances," Matthews confessed.

A third foundation of Michele's leadership was her ability to pick strong, emerging leaders and build them into a high-functioning team. Those who have worked for her talk about how they thrived under her leadership. She trusted them, gave them substantial responsibility, did not micromanage, and built a team premised on mutual respect.

By the time Michele completed her tenure as dean, she had already been courted to be president of a selective liberal arts college. She chose to stay at Wake Forest and, in the spring of 2022, was named provost. The liberal arts faculty at Wake Forest is often the most challenging and demanding within the university. She was nurtured in that culture, represented the very best of that culture, and became highly effective in calling her peers to the ideals they professed. Her life, her values, and her relationships, more than any of her words, made these appeals powerfully effective.

What I Learned

Watching Michele emerge as a leader reinforced the fact that *character matters*. Her authentic commitment to Wake Forest and its ideals knew no end. Her stated purpose in pursuing leadership was to bring differing people together around common purpose, and her life reflected what colleague Tony Marsh called a "north star moral compass." That was no mere rhetoric. I have never known anyone whose own ambition seemed so fixed on educational ideals rather than personal advancement.

If Michele has one super-gift, it is her *contagious optimism*. She admits she instinctively sees the glass half full. She encourages and affirms people, inspires confidence that there is light at the end of the tunnel, and convinces colleagues that she has their back. One colleague noted how positively she responds even when some of her own cherished dreams have been thwarted. She simply comes back the next day and asks if there are different means to achieve the same end.

Michele also shows the importance of *prizing relationships*. She cares deeply about faculty, staff, and students and always weighs the human cost of difficult decisions. An associate dean admitted that, at times, Michele's concern and empathy for others might prolong the time for a given decision. But by going the second mile to maintain relationships, Michele established a foundation of trust that buttressed her leadership in troubled times. She did not retreat from decisions that disrupted relationships, but she counted the cost in doing so.

Michele is also a great example of how *expressing genuine emotion can enhance leadership*. She was visibly moved when someone lost a parent or when a child was sick. There was not a dry eye in the room when she explained that a dear friend's son had been diagnosed with cancer. Michele shed a tear when she told her associate deans that she was moving from the dean's office to the provost's office. She was sad about breaking up a terrific team – and her colleagues welcomed the evident expression of her commitment to them.

Michele rarely shows emotion of a different kind: anger when things didn't go her way, resentment at difficult people, or exasperation when deadlines were missed. There are no stories of her having a bad day, lashing out when colleagues did not meet her standards, or complaining about mountains of work. In those contexts, Michele was generally a model of what one colleague called "compassionate accountability." But when others were hurting, troubled, or discouraged, she gave full emotional expression of her concern and commitment. That is a lesson that all of us, men and women alike, can surely learn.

Julie Freischlag

10 Julie Freischlag: Breathing Life into the Management of Medicine

I always laughingly tell the other women surgeons that Julie is the wellspring from which we've all arisen.

Betsy Tuttle
Transplant Surgeon and Chief of Surgery, East Carolina University

Julie Freischlag has been a groundbreaking surgeon and transformative medical leader and educator across the country for decades. Her record boasts an array of firsts for female surgeons: the first faculty member at the University of California–San Diego and at UCLA; the first chief of vascular surgery at UCLA; the first full professor at the Medical College of Wisconsin; and the first chair of surgery at Johns Hopkins University (Atrium Health Wake Forest Baptist, n.d.).

She has served her profession well as president of multiple surgical associations and has been lauded many times over for her contributions as a national voice for improving health care, excellence in vascular surgery, achievement in teamwork, patient safety, work–life balance, and modeling how women can succeed in the health professions (Society of University Surgeons, 2022).

My path intersected with Julie's when I co-chaired the search for a new CEO of Wake Forest Baptist and dean of Wake Forest University School of Medicine. I was struck by several things at the initial interview. First, you felt you were talking to the real Julie. She was authentic and without pretension; she gave straight answers about her career. She did not put on airs but demonstrated extensive knowledge of academic medicine, clinical practice, change management, and the modern challenges of health care.

She was laser-focused on excellence. "Whatever you choose to do," she said, "be really good at it" (Carolina Panthers, n.d.). As the first woman chair of surgery at Johns Hopkins, the highest ranked program in the country, she knew of what she spoke. Her tenure in that position required gaining trust when many traditionalists doubted her leadership. She transformed the department, making it more diverse and inclusive and bringing together different disciplines to improve patient experience and care.

Julie also loves to take on fresh challenges. Art Gibel, a trustee at Wake Forest Baptist, observed that Julie moved into an institution and quickly became "the doctor of the enterprise." She analyzed and diagnosed the situation, looked at alternate proposals that could fix the patient, chose the best one, and moved quickly to execute. "When I have to make a decision," she said in the interview, "you will never get a 'slow no.'"

The most striking takeaway from Julie's interview was her profound commitment to mentoring young surgeons, particularly women. Julie spoke of her love of teaching and how much joy and satisfaction she received from watching others develop skills and passions necessary in becoming successful surgeons. This kind of investment in others, Julie said, "gives me fuel for my soul."

When Julie became CEO of Wake Forest Baptist in 2017, she faced daunting challenges, internal and external. The center had lost millions in an unsuccessful implementation of a new computer system, and the overall financial prospects remained bleak (Davis, 2017). There was a revolving succession of senior leaders, few could see strategic momentum in the organization, and trust was at a minimum.

Wake Forest Baptist also faced stiff external competition, locally and regionally. For a decade, the administration and trustees sought to expand its footprint with acquisitions or mergers to no avail. Three other medical systems in North Carolina were larger and rapidly expanding, and questions remained as to whether Wake Forest Baptist had too small a clinical footprint to fulfill its ambition to be a highly ranked academic medical center. All in all, there was a serious morale problem within the medical center.

From day one, Julie was a whirlwind of positive energy. She rallied senior staff, showed genuine interest in faculty research, and invested heavily in leaders throughout the system.

She was everywhere in the halls of the medical school and hospital, and her message was relentlessly positive. She encouraged more than two dozen academic departments to launch public forums to present their best work; she trumpeted accomplishments of faculty, departments, and centers; she took a high profile in the community. And she maintained an active surgical practice – most recently in an internationally recognized practice in the treatment of thoracic outlet syndrome – which gives her enormous credibility among physicians.

Against the backdrop of this infectious optimism, Julie was willing to make tough decisions. Her first week on the job, she called the board chair to say she would not continue to endure a senior member of her team because of the way people were being treated. "My success has been that I can judge people . . . and I just don't have any space to work with people that aren't good people," she explained. Within a year, she replaced five department chairs, signaling that change and movement would replace the status quo.

Julie's instinct for unlocking potential was felt within the medical center. She made few changes to the senior team, which had a long history of being siloed and competitive; instead, she challenged and trusted her leaders to do their jobs. Most importantly, she drew them together as a team, discussed transparently her own strategic thinking, and listened for their feedback. She saw untapped potential in the team she inherited and went out of her way to build trusting relationships with them.

Julie also handled conflict and difficult discussions with grace. I met with her every other week and knew firsthand the thorny issues she faced. Julie would say, half in jest, "I can make a hard decision and smile while I do it." Colleagues attest to both her willingness to decide and her positive spirit in making those decisions. Part of that ability came because she did not take conflict personally; part came from an evident sense that Julie cared about people in the midst of difficult decision making.

Within a year, the board of the medical center saw dramatic change in the organization. There was a hopeful spirit, financial confidence, and new trust in the directions toward which Julie and her team pointed.

From the time I became president of Wake Forest University in 2005, the trustees and I wrestled with what to do about the modest scale of Wake Forest Baptist. While it was a more than $3 billion enterprise, with 1,200 medical school faculty and 20,000 employees, it existed in a medium-size community and had no presence in the booming regions of the state. North Carolina also had several dynamic and expanding medical systems aggressively absorbing hospitals. Wake Forest Baptist was being hemmed into a narrow base in Winston-Salem.

For a decade before Julie arrived, the medical center struggled to find adequate partners. Negotiations took place with almost every system in the Southeast, but to no avail. Julie was not deterred by any of these ill winds. She reached out to leaders of medical systems across the state with the openness and goodwill that characterized her internal efforts. Most importantly, she established a strong and transparent working relationship with Eugene Woods, the accomplished CEO of Advocate Health based in Charlotte.

In April 2019, a strategic combination was announced between Wake Forest Baptist and Atrium Health that created a combined health system with 70,000 employees, forty-two hospitals, and more than 1,500 care sites in North Carolina, South Carolina, Georgia, and Alabama. Julie was named chief academic officer for Atrium Health, and the Wake Forest University School of Medicine and Wake Forest Baptist became the academic core of Atrium Health (Berger & Faria, 2020; Berger et al., 2019).

This relationship provided great benefit to both partners. It expanded Atrium's clinical footprint, ensured the quality that academic medicine provides, and opened the opportunity to establish a medical school in Charlotte, the largest city in the country without an academic medical school (Berger & Faria, 2020). For Wake Forest, the deal provided financial stability and a future of growth that had been unimaginable.

In this new combination, Julie's responsibilities continue to expand. In December 2022, Atrium Health and Advocate Aurora Health, a major system in Chicago and Milwaukee, combined to create Advocate Health, which is based in Charlotte (Merisow & Berger, 2022). Woods serves as CEO, and Julie serves as the chief academic officer of the entire system. Advocate Health is the third largest nonprofit health system in the United States with revenues of more than $27 billion, sixty-seven hospitals, 21,000 physicians, and six million patients (Merisow & Berger, 2022). Atrium Health Wake Forest Baptist and Wake Forest University School of Medicine form the academic core of Advocate Health and are leading the way in transforming Advocate Health into an academic learning health system.

In six years leading Wake Forest Baptist, Julie has overseen remarkable transformation. She revitalized a culture, built new levels of trust and purpose throughout the organization, launched bold initiatives, and, through shrewd and careful diplomacy, assured the future of Wake Forest Baptist. From a small struggling medical system, she and her team insinuated Wake Forest into the very heart of one the largest and most dynamic medical systems in the country. What a gift of transformative leadership she has offered to Wake Forest, the local community, and now, across the broadest reaches of medical practice in the nation.

What I Learned

Knowing Julie convinced me, anew, that *leadership at the top matters*. Her enthusiasm and positive spirit were the catalysts that transformed an entire organization. She saw untapped potential throughout the medical center and cultivated it with care. It is noteworthy that, early on, Julie understood that only leaders can make durable change, and that encouraged her to take on ever-expanding roles.

Julie also refreshed my appreciation for *how important culture is to success*. She inspired people to be their best and instilled new confidence, and they trusted her instincts and decisions. It was remarkable to watch this pent-up energy released within physicians and other leaders across Wake Forest Baptist. People had a new sense that their work was important, and they were part of an organization that was on the move. Julie's positive spirit renewed a culture, and that culture unleashed a whole new wave of productive energy.

I also learned much from the *consistency* of Julie's work and messaging. She was the same in addressing trustees, the medical school faculty, and staff throughout the hospital. This consistency generated a strong foundation of trust. People heard the same message and did not conjure up ulterior motives. They had less to fear in a time of great change.

Julie may be the hardest working professional I have ever known, but *she coupled her intensity with a joyful spirit*. She loved to see medical advances in the laboratory. She loved to teach students and residents the best surgical techniques. She loved to see people cared for patiently and tenderly. She loved to see young professionals advance. In all of this, Julie embodies the kind of vocation that Frederick Buechner described as the place "where your deep gladness and the world's deep hunger meet" (Buechner, 1973).

Jonathan Lee Walton

11 Jonathan Lee Walton: Speaking with Authority

Jonathan L. Walton is one of the very few grand figures in American culture who is both public intellectual and prophetic preacher.

Cornel West
Professor Emeritus, Princeton University

In the fall of 2018, I walked across Harvard Yard to meet Jonathan Walton to try to recruit him to Wake Forest. Jonathan was Harvard University's Plummer Professor of Christian Morals and Pusey Minister in the Memorial Church (Harvard University, n.d.). I had gotten to know him when he delivered the Baccalaureate Address at Wake Forest's 2015 Commencement.

With each step in that venerable place, doubts grew about the wisdom of my venture. I thought of the vital and prestigious role that Jonathan was playing at Harvard. Why, the question reverberated in my ear, would he ever leave this special perch to come to Winston-Salem, North Carolina?

Jonathan warmly welcomed me, and we had a wonderful conversation about all he had done to befriend and engage students. I learned how Jonathan had literally and figuratively opened the doors of Memorial Chapel against the backdrop of its formal reputation. Then, I invited Jonathan to come to Wake Forest as a senior leader with multiple roles, a distinguished scholar, dean of the divinity school, dean of Wait Chapel, and a member of the president's cabinet.

Jonathan listened carefully, and we had a long and engaged conversation about the kinds of roles that he could play on campus. He showed more interest in the position than I might have imagined, and we agreed to continue the conversation. In the fall of 2019, Jonathan accepted the invitation to come to Wake Forest (Batten & Walker, 2019).

I had a keen interest in Jonathan for two reasons: the power of his preaching and his grounded leadership. He is a powerful speaker, very much in the vein of notable Black preachers like Martin Luther King, Jr. and Andrew Young. Like them, he grew up in Atlanta where his life was inextricably bound with communities of faith. He grew up in what he recalls "as a beautifully enchanted world."

This world included heroes. When Jonathan was in elementary school, he remembers his father picking him up early to attend the unveiling of the statue of Hank Aaron at Fulton County Stadium. At the ceremony, his father introduced him to the legendary president of Morehouse College, Benjamin Elijah Mays. Much later, Jonathan and his wife, Cecily, would choose to name one of their sons Elijah Mays.

This world also included mentors. Jonathan was nurtured by ministers such as Reverend William Smith, Kenneth Samuel, and Gerald Durley, and Morehouse College ministers like Dr. Lawrence Carter, founding dean of the Martin Luther King Jr. International Chapel (Morehouse College, n.d.). Jonathan was also encouraged to speak in church, even as a college student, by many in the congregation. They affirmed his gift and, as he confesses, did not judge him by who he was at the time but by his potential.

This world was also replete with biblical characters and powerful stories. "I learned the meaning of moral courage from Moses, integrity from Esther, the danger of absolute power from David and Solomon. The Bible was a rich tapestry of life-giving stories." Like King, Jonathan believed the Word of God had power to change hearts of stone (Lischer, 1997). "The overall message of the Bible," Jonathan later said, shows us that "grace is more noble than greed, inclusion more honorable than envy, compassion more Christ-like than covetousness, intellect more prized than ignorance, faith more enduring than fear, and hope is more life-giving than hostility" (Walton, 2018).

After starting to preach in college, Jonathan continued to develop his craft at Princeton Theological Seminary, earning both master's and doctoral degrees. It was during that time that he also wrestled with whether he wanted to be a preacher or a scholar. In a paper he was writing for Professor Cornel West, Jonathan strove to write in an erudite fashion – extended paragraphs, complex sentences, sophisticated words. West called him into his office and said, "Now brother, I've heard you speak, and you are such an effective communicator. But I don't see it here. . . . What is your process when you are writing a sermon?"

Jonathan answered that he took a yellow legal pad and began playing with phrases, projecting ideas, and turning them into sentences. Then he would string ideas into paragraphs and work together toward a climax. "Now take this paper and go do that," West responded. "Don't be afraid to write for the ear." Reflecting on that experience, Jonathan noted, "Everything I've ever written, two books, dozens of articles, have all been written in that way."

Jonathan excels as a religiously inspired orator, fully embodying Cicero's threefold purposes of a speech: to teach, delight, and move. Even his invocations and benedictions are striking and have become legendary at both Harvard and Wake Forest. In less than two minutes, he can capture attention, warm the heart, and drive home an important message. A good example is his benediction and charge to the graduates before some 30,000 people at the 2015 Harvard Commencement.

> Go in peace, speak the truth. Give thanks for each day. Be quick to compliment liberally. Learn to love out loud. Be slow to criticize. And if you do so, do so discreetly and constructively. Love yourself, for loving yourself is a precondition for loving your neighbor. Realize in the words of Bryan Stevenson, each of us is more than the worst act we've ever committed. Yet be humble enough to realize that none of us is as good as the best thing we will ever accomplish. Live simply. Be of service. Give yourself to a cause bigger than yourself. And when we do these things, we will begin to approximate what it means to do justice, to love mercy and to walk humbly before our God. Amen (Walton, 2015).

At the end of this prayer, Professor Diana Eck, one of the commentators for the online video of the service, noted, with evident surprise: "Wow, even some applause for the prayer" (Walton, 2015).

Jonathan is a powerful preacher due to the force of his convictions, his ability to draw in an audience, and a compelling rhetorical style nurtured in the finest traditions of African-American preaching. He constructs stories and captures vivid images. Mostly, Jonathan has important things to say; his messages are not merely rhetorical performances. He presents compelling moral challenges, deeply personal words of affirmation and comfort, and guidance in navigating the complexities of modern life. No one in the audience feels exempt from his gaze and the impact of his words.

Jonathan's description of his own preaching strategy is straightforward. "Be personal. Sincere. Put a face on all and humanize everyone (friend and foe, hero and villain alike). And move toward an unexpected conclusion."

In one memorable address, "Laying Our Hammers Down," Jonathan spoke about his father, John Henry Walton, who had recently passed away. He began with the folk legend John Henry – a steel-driving man with a 40-pound hammer and Herculean strength. Competing with a steam-powered drill to finish a railroad tunnel, John Henry beat the mechanical drill with superhuman effort, and laid down his hammer and died. He refused to give up the race until he declared victory.

"My father," Jonathan intoned, "lived up to the legend of John Henry." He struck an intimidating pose and seemed to carry the weight of the world on his broad shoulders. In one five-year period, to support his family, he literally worked around the clock.

In a brilliant twist, Jonathan reversed the lesson one would expect him to make. Instead of calling for hard work and endurance, he suggested its very opposite. John Henry Walton retired and in the last twenty years of his life was able to teach life's more important lessons: love and beauty, time with grandchildren, "sitting next to him on a porch in North Carolina, singing James Cleveland gospel classics." His advice to Jonathan, and by extension to the Harvard audience of well-groomed achievers, was to invest less in work, not more. "He laid down his hammer so that he could pick up life and pick up love. He wants me to tell you this morning to go and do likewise" (Walton, 2018).

Jonathan commands authority when he mounts the pulpit, speaking with a deep, resonant voice. Yet his demeanor is also winsome and approachable. As his Wake Forest colleague Reid Morgan noted, "He pulls you in … and makes you glad to be challenged. He has an exceptional ability to make you want to take your ideals and do more with them."

Jonathan's appeal as a leader also springs from the fact that his life readily parallels his words. In his leadership capacities, he has shown tremendous attention to treating everyone as children of God, particularly the most vulnerable. At Harvard, he went out of his way to welcome students who might be struggling. At Wake Forest, Jonathan led the divinity school through a major curriculum reform, opened Wait Chapel for more services, and launched the COMPASS Initiative, which helps prepare ministry leaders to address needs of vulnerable populations (Wake Forest University, n.d.).

As a transformative leader, Jonathan has very strong religious, moral, and political convictions, but he exudes a rare care and concern for everyone and sustains friendships across the political spectrum. At Harvard and Wake Forest, he played a signal role as the institutions reckoned with complicated issues of race and justice in the era of Black Lives Matter. Jonathan had strong and progressive views on these matters but, in the words of Harvard President Emerita Drew Faust, always remained an "honest broker" in bridging the university and faculty and student concerns. At Wake Forest, he played an indispensable role in helping the university come to terms with its antebellum history.

Anyone who receives an email or letter from Jonathan will find that he signs it "One Luv." He says he spells L-U-V because he says he considers himself a "Southern hip-hop cat who has a bit of a flair." But One Luv comes from the words of Benjamin Elijah Mays, the great preacher and educator, who said, "The love of God and the love of humanity are one love" (Henson, 2020). That single message is one that Jonathan Walton's life has proclaimed in word and deed.

What I Learned

Jonathan always has something important to say. Whatever the occasion, he invests enough time and thought in preparation that his words are appealing and forceful – never just off the cuff. Jonathan honors his audience by the seriousness he shows in speaking to them. I learned that *words can have power but it takes creative and sustained effort to make them so.*

Jonathan illustrates the power of the adage that *people don't care what you think unless they know that you care.* He relates to people with genuine curiosity and connection. His messages seem real because that kind of genuine care is evident.

Jonathan's messages can be prophetic, particularly in attacking callousness to the plight of the poor, the immigrant, the prisoner, the child in poverty. He starts where people are and shows why silence on these issues contradicts their own cherished values. From Jonathan I learned *you have to reason with, not just denounce, those with whom you disagree* (Walton, 2018).

Jonathan also lived the *importance of family and friendship*. He told me that a main reason he found Wake Forest attractive was that we took his family seriously. What would be best for Cecily and his three children? Jonathan speaks and writes brilliantly, but he lives in a way that shows what is most important in life is love, family, community, and connection.

Michael Lamb

12 Michael Lamb: Reimagining Character in Higher Education

Michael always starts with people in mind. People are at the front of all his motivation, all of his decisions.

Ann Phelps
Director of Programming for Leadership and Character, Wake Forest University

I was introduced to Michael Lamb by Wake Forest graduate Jim O'Connell, who was studying at Oxford University as a Rhodes Scholar. Out of the blue, Jim called me and said there was a young scholar that I needed to meet. Jim was in an ethics discussion group at Oxford led by Michael and believed there was an overlap of common interests – particularly how character should be woven into liberal arts education, an issue of vital interest at Wake Forest.

A former Rhodes Scholar himself, Michael returned to Oxford after earning a doctorate in political theory. He helped launch the Oxford Character Project, which asked graduate students to consider the role of ethics in their professions. He also was dean of leadership, service, and character development at Rhodes House and, in that capacity, engaged Jim and other Rhodes Scholars (Wake Forest University, n.d.).

What impressed Jim most about Michael was not his brilliance and unparalleled success. Instead, it was his interest in making deep, meaningful friendships. At Oxford, where students stack credentials and strive for status and acclaim, Michael focused on human connections. He challenged students to reflect on what really mattered in life – to sort out their true motivations and ambitions. "Many of us found him to be a kind of port in the storm," Jim said.

A few months later, in the summer of 2015, Michael was workshopping his book manuscript in North Carolina, and we arranged a breakfast meeting. I had long dreamed of a new scholarship program at Wake Forest that focused on character development. Michael and I brainstormed about how such a program might be designed. Six months later, we invited Michael to come to Wake Forest for an extensive visit – both of us evaluating whether such a program was feasible and whether he might be the appropriate leader. In the summer of 2016, we welcomed Michael to Wake Forest with the challenge of envisaging and developing a signature program in leadership and character.

From the start, nothing was certain. We didn't have a clear blueprint to follow, we had no funding on hand, and we knew we would need to build partnerships with faculty. And across the sweep of American higher education there were few models to emulate. But I was convinced we had the right leader. Risks and all, we moved forward.

Michael grew up on a farm in Chapel Hill, Tennessee, a town of a couple thousand people 50 miles south of Nashville. His parents were active leaders in this face-to-face community, and Michael inherited habits of long hours and diligent work, responsibility for neighbors, and the importance of education. Neither of his parents had graduated from college, but they impressed upon him two things: the great value of a college degree and the financial reality that a scholarship would be necessary to fulfill that dream. Accordingly, Michael excelled in school and blossomed as a natural leader: a two-sport athlete serving as student body president in junior high, president of his local Future Farmers of America and Beta Club in high school, and delegate to Boys State in Tennessee, where he won a speaking contest.

One reason that Michael became passionate about character development was that his own college experience was so transformative. He entered Rhodes College in Memphis as the recipient of two major scholarships, one academic and one focused on service. At Rhodes, his record was nothing short of stunning.

Michael was relentlessly curious, throwing himself into the study of politics and American history, religion, philosophy, and ethics. What galvanized his study was something outside the classroom: the ten hours of leadership and service that he contributed each week as part of his service scholarship – working at a homeless shelter, tutoring students, building houses for Habitat for Humanity – and his reflections upon that experience.

In 2004, Michael was awarded a Rhodes Scholarship to study philosophy and theology at Oxford (Michael Lamb, n.d.). An early experience in a tutorial session there clarified what would become one of his deepest commitments: He would not settle for detached learning. Writing a paper for a distinguished professor on the problem of evil, Michael opened with descriptions of the horrendous 2004 tsunami in the Indian Ocean. "Excellent arguments," his professor said in his critique. "But I didn't like the first paragraph about the tsunami in Asia. It's not properly detached for an essay in philosophy." Michael took strong exception to this vein of thought: "Philosophy must enliven – and be enlivened by – engagement with everyday experience" (Lamb, 2007).

In the fall of 2009, Michael entered a doctoral program in political theory at Princeton, where he continued to excel. Taking a broad range of courses in politics, philosophy, and religion, he came to focus on the study of Augustine and the theme of hope. His revised dissertation on that subject has now been published as a Princeton University Press book, *A Commonwealth of Hope: Augustine's Political Thought* (2022). He also excelled in teaching, winning the George Kateb Preceptor Award from Princeton's Department of Politics (Michael Lamb, n.d.).

He also was known as a leader among his peers. His academic advisor said that Michael was one of the two or three best leaders he had seen in twenty-five years of graduate teaching. He also noted that at Michael's dissertation defense, the faculty committee joked beforehand that Michael might well become a college president even before his six- to seven-year path to tenure.

In the middle of his doctoral work, Michael took off a year and a half to work in campaign politics. He had long known Roy Herron, a legendary Tennessee State senator, who began a campaign for governor before becoming the 2010 Democratic candidate for Congress from Tennessee's 8th District. Michael served as chief of staff for both campaigns with their eighty-hour weeks, relentless fundraising, and door-to-door canvassing. Herron lost the race, and Michael found the experience deeply disconcerting – particularly the lack of character he witnessed in many throughout the political sphere.

He returned to finish his doctorate at Princeton thinking more of a vocation in teaching and writing. "If I found ways to connect political theory, philosophy, and ethics with actual formation and education that aims toward leadership and citizenship, then I might turn out many future citizens and leaders who could help shape our democracy."

Over the last six years at Wake Forest, Michael has built the Program for Leadership and Character in a way that is remarkable in its conception, execution, and appeal. He has created a novel program – in many ways countercultural to modern academic culture, which has largely avoided intentional efforts to form the character of university students. The effort at Wake Forest is a bold attempt to recover and reimagine character education in a pluralistic context.

The program began with a clear conviction that character development could and should be taught in an academically rigorous way. It is premised on seven methods of character development from philosophy that have received empirical support from scholars in education, psychology, and the social sciences. Those methods include "habituation through practice, reflection on personal experience, engagement with virtuous exemplars, dialogue that increases virtue literacy, awareness of situational influences and cognitive biases, moral reminders that make norms salient, and friendships of mutual support and accountability" (Lamb et al., 2021).

The scale and depth of the Program for Leadership and Character is nothing short of breathtaking. Over $60 million has been committed to its expansion by Wake Forest donors and a set of national foundations. The program, which now employs around forty people, has seen growth in five major areas (Walker, 2023).

First, Wake Forest has developed extensive student programming, including a new Leadership and Character Scholars program that recruits ten to twelve new students per year to attend the university free of charge. In return, scholars agree to participate in specially designed programming, community engagement, and research. The first class of these scholars graduated in 2023.

Second, the program has worked to embed issues of character across the curriculum by offering grants to help faculty deepen their expertise in character development and generate new courses or revise existing courses better to support students' growth as human beings and leaders of character.

Third, leadership and character development has expanded into professional education, especially law and medicine. The program, supported by the Kern Family Foundation, guides and supports students, residents, and professionals in developing relevant virtues, such as compassion, justice, resilience, and wisdom in their lives and work.

Fourth, the program has established a cutting-edge research program, which includes efforts to evaluate the success of its courses and programs. The John Templeton Foundation is supporting these efforts in research and evaluation. The program has also hosted several major conferences with the Oxford Character Project.

Fifth, and most recently, the program has taken on national dimensions. A grant from Lilly Endowment Inc. will allow Wake Forest to award grants to other colleges and universities to create their own initiatives focused on character education. This will forge a national network of colleges and universities that can educate a new generation of ethically grounded leaders (Walker, 2023).

Michael's leadership has been remarkable in three respects. First, in seven years, he has worked to embed the Program for Leadership and Character deeply into the culture of Wake Forest. Remarkably, he's done so until recently as an assistant professor, receiving tenure only in the spring of 2023. He now holds the F. M. Kirby Foundation Chair of Leadership and Character.

Second, he has been recognized as a national leader whose work can serve as leaven for character education within higher education. His efforts in teaching and mentoring, undergraduate and professional education, and research and writing have established plausible models for others to emulate.

His third great achievement is that he has accomplished all of this while avoiding the riptide of polarization that has characterized American public life – and university life – in recent years. The program bridges various kinds of difference. It has welcomed diverse voices into conversation and avoided being boxed in as too liberal or conservative, too secular or religious. It has focused on issues of the common good and challenged students to live lives of purpose and meaning with courage and humility – according to their own values and with deep respect for others. Students of all political and religious stripes have flourished in the program, and individual donors – left, right, and center – have applauded the program's efforts.

What I Learned

I have never known anyone who better *exemplified the examined life* – a life enriched by ongoing reflection and deliberation. The overflow of this passion is that students both learn about virtues and then are inspired to live accordingly. Living the moral life is an abiding quest for Michael and one that he yearns to impart.

Michael has the rare gift of *probing with students the deepest issues of the heart*. He cracks open the veneer that most students put forward and invites them to describe and explain their deepest needs and motivations. Students yearn to be real with each other, and the Program for Leadership and Character promotes contexts for this transparency to take root. I am reminded that transparency and vulnerability are the richest seedbed for virtuous living.

He is one of the *most driven and most personable people* I have known. He thinks and writes at a world-class level and is driven to accomplish an incredible array of projects. At the same time, he values relationships and friendships above all else. Teaching and mentoring students is what gives him the greatest pleasure, and many seek his counsel about the most profound issues in their lives. Michael reminds me that deep friendship and outstanding accomplishment can both flourish in the same person.

Michael is completely *comfortable in his own skin*. He has never forgotten where he came from and is not embarrassed by his Southern accent or rural, working-class background. At the same time, he does not parade his Princeton and Oxford credentials to distinguish himself from others. Students from any and every background are drawn to him. He is a model of excellence without pretension, a wonderful lesson for anyone in higher education.

Dave Clawson

13 Dave Clawson: Building a Sports Team of Excellence and Character

Clawson has proved he could be successful at a lot of places. But he also has shown he doesn't necessarily prioritize what other coaches prioritize.

Andy Staples
Senior Writer, The Athletic
(Staples, 2022)

I almost blew the recruitment of Dave Clawson as football coach to Wake Forest. In December 2013, Ron Wellman, Wake Forest's athletic director, and I attended the championship game of the Mid-America Athletic Conference between Northern Illinois and Dave's team, Bowling Green (Associated Press, 2013). The following day, we planned to ask Dave to throw in his lot with Wake Forest.

We were supposed to be at the game anonymously, not revealing who we were or why we were there. The game had hardly started before the plan fell apart. On their first play from scrimmage, Bowling Green completely outfoxed the defense, leaving a receiver wide open for a 30-yard gain. I was so excited I jumped up and began cheering. Wellman grabbed my arm and reminded me of the ground rules – anonymity. Thereafter, I tried to restrain myself as Dave's team, behind an ingeniously deceptive offense, rolled up the score against the favored, sixteenth-ranked Northern Illinois team (Associated Press, 2013).

Witnessing that strategic ingenuity was a wonderful introduction to Dave Clawson. When he came to Wake Forest in 2013, in his mid-forties, he had already been a transformative head coach for three different programs – Fordham, Richmond, and Bowling Green (Hale, 2021; Wake Forest University, n.d.). In all three cases, he took struggling programs and built conference champions.

Through the recruitment process, we learned Dave was a patient program builder. There was no quick fix to a program that had gone 4–8 the previous season and won only two games in the Atlantic Coast Conference (ACC). Dave's priority was building the right team culture, not just winning games. Team culture was first. Success would follow – in time.

That is the course of Dave's tenure over the last decade at Wake Forest. The team had a losing record the first two years. Since then, they played in seven straight bowl games, winning five. In 2021, they boasted an 11–3 record, 7–1 in the ACC, and won the conference's Atlantic Division, and Dave was named ACC Coach of the Year. His combined two-year record for the 2021 and 2022 seasons was 19–8 (Wake Forest University, n.d.).

Dave embodies the ideals of intercollegiate sports: excellence in competition, commitment to collegiate education and graduation, and character development. At a time when competitive success has overwhelmed all else and scandals have rocked college sports, Dave has retained an unflinching commitment to academics and leadership development as bedrocks of his program.

I once asked Dave why he went into coaching after he graduated from Williams College when most of his friends were headed to law school or Wall Street. Dave, a politics and economics major who played both basketball and football in college, told me there was a power and satisfaction of being on a team that he didn't want to give up. So, he opted for the hand-to-mouth existence of a novice football coach – spending two years at Buffalo, three years at Lehigh, and three years at Villanova.

Dave's leadership incorporates his intelligence and drive for excellence, his deeply personal approach to staff and students, his unswerving steadiness, and his great communication skills.

First, Dave is smart, intense, and inquisitive. Kevin Higgins, who has coached with Dave for two decades, said, "He has this unique ability to ask the right question, get an answer, and do something with the answer. He's got this inquisitive mind that can get to the heart of situations very quickly."

His high expectations for himself extend to others, which can be something of a culture shock for younger players and staff. Yet Dave is willing to honestly confront when expectations aren't met. John Wolford, a former star quarterback at Wake Forest who spent two years with the Los Angeles Rams, said that Dave tells the unvarnished truth. He "opts for the hard answer," not taking the easy way out, because he knows a problem never gets better by avoiding it.

Dave is also highly relational and deeply interested in people. He sets standards and equitably administers them; he listens and takes advice; he seeks to give staff ownership of the program. He takes family issues seriously, giving staff a schedule a full year in advance so vacations can be planned. A football program is well over 200 people, and Dave strives to know each one of them. Evidence of this commitment is the loyalty and continuity among his staff, which is unmatched in college football. Offensive coordinator Warren Ruggiero, offensive line coach Nick Tabacca, and running backs coach John Hunter have all worked with Dave for a decade or more.

Dave is also steady and consistent. There are football coaches who rant and rave, who give spellbinding speeches to their teams in the vein of Knute Rockne. That's not Dave. His approach is analytical, not emotional. "He is the same person every day, whether we win by 40, lose by 40," said Dave Cohen, assistant head coach for defense. There's not a lot of rah-rah on the sidelines. "Coach Clawson is not screaming at us when we get a three and out; he's not running down the sidelines when we score a touchdown," said quarterback Sam Hartman during a postgame press conference on October 1, 2022. "He's Coach Clawson. He's an even-keeled guy. We reflect that in the way we play."

Dave's consistency stabilizes the whole program. Assistant coaches say it helps them be consistent with players and orients young football players. "He treats every player the same," Cohen added, "whether they've been here a week or been here five or six years. It's consistent for the star of the team or the benchwarmer."

Dave's leadership is also rooted in his belief that great communication empowers organizations. When staff and players understand what is happening, they can embrace the program as their own. In person, in print and online, in group meetings and one-on-one interactions, the Wake Forest football program is deeply connected. Dave's regular meetings with coaches include support staff – up to sixty people – so that "people understand where they fit and what we're trying to achieve as a program," Dave explained.

Each year, Dave and his staff craft a policy manual for the program, spelling out in intricate detail expectations, schedules, and consequences for violating team standards – keeping everyone on the same page. He also establishes mechanisms to ensure that communication with the team is not just top-down. During the season, he meets every Monday morning for breakfast with team captains, asking what issues he needs to be aware of and what players need some extra attention. "Who are the guys we need to put our arms around?" he asks. "I can fix zero percent of the problems I don't know about."

How did Dave build a successful football program at Wake Forest – the smallest school in a Power 5 conference, a place that one sportswriter deemed the "worst job" in big-time college football? (Haney, 2015). He has done it in unconventional ways, exploiting Wake Forest's assets, not its liabilities. Sportswriter David Hale compares this approach to "moneyball," building a team around different metrics of evaluating players and different gametime strategies (Hale, 2021).

One example is the recruitment of quarterbacks. Both Wolford and Hartman, standouts at Wake Forest, were undersized and unattractive to other Power 5 teams. But Dave saw devilishly smart, competitive, and devoted students of the game who could orchestrate a complex offense. Both players claimed multiple victories, set school and conference records, won bowl games, and, in Wolford's case, has played in the NFL with the Los Angeles Rams.

"We're not beating Clemson, Alabama, Georgia, or Ohio State for quarterbacks," Dave said. "The one thing we've been willing to sacrifice is height. They must be curious and passionate, instinctual and studious, able to process – but they don't have to be tall" (Raynor, 2023).

Dave and his longtime offensive coordinator, Warren Ruggiero, have also engineered a unique – often baffling – offense called the "slow mesh." The quarterback does not quickly hand off the ball to the running back, but they stand together – "the mesh" – for as many as two and a half seconds. This scheme keeps the defense guessing whether the play will be a run or pass, often forcing them to question their basic instincts. If they are undecided or guess wrong, Wake Forest's quarterback reads the weakness and exploits it.

Dave's approach is counter to typical expectations. Instead of focusing exclusively on athletic talent, giving only lip service to issues of character, he believes a team of character has a better opportunity to win.

He sets the tone for his program from the time he meets recruits and their families. The message is simple: Come to Wake Forest if you love football, want to complete a quality college education, and are committed to developing as a leader of character. The culture reinforces these values day in and day out.

Proof of concept in Dave's overall approach is that recent football success has gone hand-in-hand with higher academic performance, overall grade point average, and the highest graduation success in Wake Forest football history – 93 percent compared to a national average of 76 percent (Pantages, 2022).

Dave has also executed a careful plan of leadership formation. His comprehensive evaluation system, applied to all 100 players, invites players to evaluate themselves – on their football prowess, aspects of character, issues of leadership, and performance in the classroom. Then each player receives an in-person evaluation with five adults: the head coach, defensive or offensive coordinator, position coach, strength coach, and academic advisor. There is frank discussion about where the player stands and what goals should be established for the coming year.

Additionally, Dave developed explicit leadership training for his Leadership Council – a group of sixteen players, elected by their teammates, that represent all classes and positions. In the spring term, Dave meets weekly with them to discuss leadership books. Players lead the conversation, and Dave poses questions that analyze good and effective leadership. From this group, coaches choose team captains for the coming season.

The Leadership Council is also a bridge between coaches and players. They apply their lessons in leadership to improve the culture and performance of the team. Dave is convinced that football success will occur when a critical mass of players is self-motivated to improve and push themselves beyond what they are told to do – when together, they take charge and convince each other of what it takes to excel.

Contrary to the emphasis of other collegiate coaches, Dave places competitive sport in the larger context of educational opportunity and leadership development. He will do everything possible to launch his best players into the NFL, but his larger gift is to hundreds of student athletes whom he has prepared for life, helped to grow in maturity, and inspired to succeed wherever their dreams may lead.

What I Learned

Dave taught me that *to build or renew the culture of an organization takes time, persistence, and courage*. Obstacles, however numerous and unexpected, must be addressed. When Dave arrived at Wake Forest, he wanted to ensure that younger players were attending all classes and asked staff members to check on them. Some faculty objected; this had never been done and was overly intrusive. Dave attended a faculty meeting, explained his rationale, and outlined how class attendance was part of a larger plan for player development. Hearing him out, the faculty readily accepted the plan.

I learned anew *the value of hiring staff with the same core values*. Dave has not built a distinct culture by himself. His staff, many of whom have been together for years, sing off the same song sheet. Therefore, players do not receive mixed messages about expectations on the gridiron or on campus.

Dave illustrates that *great leadership involves a relentless quest for excellence*. I have never talked to Dave without learning of the next challenge he is addressing, the next goal toward which he is striving. He is inquisitive, always looking for the next competitive edge.

Dave showed that *one can be intensely competitive and gracious at the same time*. There is nothing more competitive than college football, but Dave modulates that drive to win with an equally intense commitment to do things the right way. He tells players that football is important but never more important than faith, family, and doing the right thing.

Don Flow

14 Don Flow: Advancing the Well-Being of the City

Don Flow is without question the most thoroughly read and intellectually sophisticated businessman I have ever met. ... He's always curious. He's always learning.

James Hunter
Distinguished Professor, University of Virginia

I knew Don Flow by reputation when I came to Wake Forest in 2005. We had mutual friends who encouraged us to get together, so we met for lunch in my first weeks in Winston-Salem, and there seemed no end to our common interests – from theology to politics, history to academic life, business conditions to the nature of leadership.

It might seem odd for a new university president to seek out a local automobile dealer, but Don is no typical car salesman. When Julie Freischlag, the current CEO of Wake Forest Baptist Health, first met Don, she worried that they might have nothing to talk about. Instead, she later confessed, the person she encountered was a "renaissance man."

Don grew up in Winston-Salem, the son of successful Volkswagen dealer and community leader. He was an all-state running back and went to the University of Virginia on a football scholarship.

When I asked Don when he first thought of himself as a leader, he said it was his junior year of high school. In the first wave of integrating Winston-Salem schools, the junior and senior classes of three high schools – one that had been all black and one all white – were thrown together into a single school. Building athletic teams in this environment became a huge problem. In the face of these challenges, Don's football coach came to him and asked, "How are we going to do this? Given all the racial issues involved, help me develop a single, unified team."

At the University of Virginia, Don excelled as a student, and the athletic director encouraged him to become involved in student government. At the end of his junior year, he was awarded the Arthur Gray Scholarship for the outstanding student leader at the university. During his senior year, Don was one of two students chosen to visit privately with Queen Elizabeth and Prince Philip when they visited the university to celebrate the United States' bicentennial.

After college, Don fully intended to return home and work in the family business. But he was also a serious person of faith and decided to seek a graduate degree in theology. Those studies, combined with his later MBA from Wake Forest University, set a distinct pattern in Don's life: a quest to think theologically and philosophically about business and capitalism and to build a corporation based on this vision and these principles.

Don spent his first four years in the car business working every job in the dealership – beginning as a service mechanic. "I wanted to come side-by-side with everybody who has done the job" (Duke University Divinity School, 2010).

In managing his first dealership, Don sought to rethink and reformulate the car business – to write a fresh mission statement for the business. One crusty mechanic told him that all that philosophizing about how better to serve customers was simply "bullshit." A year later when Don asked him the same question, the mechanic said he still had his questions about all that talk but the increase in service business had lifted his income by 50 percent. That year Flow Honda won an award as the outstanding Honda dealership in the country.

Don's wife, Robbin, once said that for Don the cup is never just half full. "It's like full," she said. "He has all this positive energy. I love the way that he always sees possibilities where others see obstacles" (Wake Forest University, n.d.). Don's dynamic presence comprises a set of creative tensions. He is a person of action *and* deep reflection. He is driven *and* deeply caring. He brims with confidence *and* humility. He is a defender of capitalism *and* a serious critic of unrestrained capitalism. And he is a person of deep Christian faith *and* a leader working for the common good across political, racial, and religious lines. He has been described as "a North Star, always telling the truth, always being transparent about what is going on, and always being willing to listen to the other side of the story."

For the last forty years, Don has applied his gifts to building an iconic automobile business that includes fifty-three dealerships in North Carolina and Virginia, with more than 2,000 employees, representing over twenty manufacturers – from General Motors to Ford, Honda to Toyota, BMW to Audi and Mercedes. Flow Automotive Companies has won every conceivable award from these companies.

The scale of Flow Automotive Companies is impressive. More striking is the way it does business. Over time, Don deconstructed everything about selling and servicing cars to make Flow Automotive a purpose-driven, people-centric, community-engaged company. "Our organization is built on three foundational commitments that define why we exist, what we want to be, and how we want to work together," Don stated in an internal statement of leadership philosophy. These commitments include:

(1) Covenant with our customers to be a place that keeps its promises and is worthy of their trust.
(2) Community with one another working toward a common vision.
(3) Commitment to enhancing the common good of every city where we do business (Flow, n.d.).

The most radical commitment is to the customer. "If we have a covenant relationship with this customer," Don said, "if we are to treat them like a valued friend, what would every interaction look like?" In a training program inside the company, the following questions are asked: "Would you send your mother or daughter, unaccompanied, to buy a car?" "Would you go home to the dinner table tonight and tell every person at your table exactly what you did and said today?"

To build this culture of trust and transparency, Flow Automotive Companies breaks with typical automobile sales techniques. The company sets a standard price for everyone and does not negotiate, putting all customers on the same playing field. Sales staff do not have an economic incentive to sell a car for a higher price. Warren Buffett – himself a significant investor in automobile dealerships – has spoken publicly about this distinct "Flow" approach, one "which emphasizes fixed prices, transparency and low sales pressure" (Buffett & Munger, 2017).

Flow Automotive Companies also has a deep commitment to its employees. Don speaks of re-personalizing the workplace. "There are no little people, and there is no ordinary work" (Duke University Divinity School, 2010). Don speaks of a culture of "high caring, high challenge." He holds "members" of the organization to high standards, but the company also takes care of them in wholistic ways – in benefits and health care, reasonable work schedules, college scholarships for their children, financial literacy courses, and a crisis emergency fund. Employees are given paid time off to volunteer in the community, many working together to build houses for Habitat for Humanity (Duke University Divinity School, 2010).

Don and the company are also deeply committed to the common good of the communities in which they operate. In making these investments, Don criticizes "agency theory," which suggests that return for investors is the primary, or only, concern of management (Bower & Paine, 2017). "We think about our communities as cultural banks where the social, intellectual, aesthetic, political, and economic capital from the past has been deposited and is available to be drawn down to meet the present need" (Flow Leadership Philosophy). Don argues that his company and its leaders have a responsibility to reinvest in all of these sectors, to strengthen the common good for the next generation. On several occasions, Don has refused to sell Flow because he wants to sustain these commitments. Not since Max De Pree in the 1990s has anyone expressed so clearly and thoughtfully the moral purposes of a business and attempted to put those human-centered values into practice (O'Toole, 2019).

Beyond his business interests, Don has played the galvanizing role in the redevelopment of Winston-Salem, a city challenged by the loss of textile and tobacco manufacturing and the departure of two major banks to Charlotte. Repeatedly, Don's relentless enthusiasm built coalitions to renew the city and region. He spends as much as half of his time on projects for community development.

Some twenty years ago, he was instrumental in forming "The Millennium Fund," in which individuals, corporations, and organizations pulled together to raise more than $53 million to invest in the future of Winston-Salem. During that time, the change in the city has been remarkable, from a place to avoid to a thriving destination. The fund transformed the tallest, but derelict, building into a high-end apartment complex, invested in a new minor league baseball stadium, and added the Goler Community Development Corporation, a major African-American initiative.

More recently, Don purchased another abandoned eighteen-story downtown building, formerly owned by GMAC Insurance. The $20 million renovation project provided new offices for his own company and two floors to launch an entrepreneurial hub for the city. "Winston-Starts" is an accelerator that provides wonderful space and mentoring for start-up companies.

The most audacious civic challenge Don has undertaken was the redevelopment of Whitaker Park – a 220-acre manufacturing complex that Reynolds American Tobacco was leaving. In 2015, Reynolds offered the property to a newly formed not-for-profit that Don chaired. For tax reasons, the property could not be developed for five years, and for many reasons, most leaders in the community deemed the financial risks too great. Almost alone, Don argued to move forward. He personally launched an effort to raise an investment fund, and in a week's time, individuals and institutions in the community pledged $13 million to an at-risk investment fund.

Over the last five years, the Whitaker Park development has prospered beyond anyone's – except Don's – expectations. More than $100 million of private capital has been invested, all invested funds have been repaid with interest, and the nonprofit has ended up with $14 million in economic development funds. Today, there are over 1,000 jobs in Whitaker Park. It was a team effort but would not have happened without Don's determined persistence.

Don has also been active in initiatives to address intergenerational poverty and racial disparities. He has helped provide additional support for public education, particularly to enhance reading for elementary students. He also initiated a minority business grant program during the COVID pandemic that has given grants to over forty minority businesses in Winston-Salem. Bishop Sir Walter Mack, Jr., a leading African-American in Winston-Salem, has noted Don's ability "to rally people together from all spectrums of life."

Don has also played a pivotal role at Wake Forest University. One of my first moves as president was to recruit him as a trustee, and we have been serious collaborators on many projects. From 2015 to 2018, he chaired the Wake Forest University Board of Trustees, including a successful billion-dollar capital campaign. He has also chaired the board of the Wake Forest Baptist Medical Center where his influence has been instrumental, first in bringing together Wake Forest Medical School and the North Carolina Baptist Hospital, and later in merging Wake Forest Baptist Health, a system of five hospitals, with Atrium Health in Charlotte with over forty hospitals.

A decade ago, Don was also the primary organizer to bring the ATP World 250 men's tennis tournament to Winston-Salem and the campus of Wake Forest. The Winston-Salem Open at Wake Forest, the last stop in August before the US Open, has been a great success. And the wonderful set of courts and facilities built by the tournament has been a major factor in the success of collegiate tennis at Wake Forest, with its men's team winning the NCAA championship in 2018.

What I Learned

Don is a person with a *deeply integrated philosophy of life*. His choices, personal and professional, spring from his deep Christian convictions, thorough identification with his community, knowledge of how social change takes place, and abiding vision to build a community that flourishes for all its citizens. I have never known anyone whose actions seem to derive so much from his core convictions.

I also learned a great deal about *humility and generosity* from Don. People have come to trust Don because his own ego seems so little in play. He is trusted by people who are progressives and conservatives, religious and secular, black and white. Don and Robbin do nothing to flaunt wealth, station, or accomplishment. They are also generous beyond measure as almost any social service agency in Winston-Salem can attest. All of this is done without fanfare, often anonymously – the left hand not knowing what the right hand is doing.

Don is always *striving for a bigger vision.* In whatever context, he pushes for new possibilities, raising expectations, and facing the future with courage and fortitude. Watching Don strive, year after year, to build a flourishing community, sometimes against overwhelming odds, is to witness a person who lives in hope.

I also learned from Don about *the meaning of friendship.* He was always a safe confidant, a loyal supporter, and someone who could straighten out my thinking when it veered to one side or another. We profited by reading many of the same articles and books and reflecting often on the moral purposes of higher education. Often, I was as much pupil as teacher.

Conclusion

Universities today are wonderful and complicated places. They continue to play an oversized role in our culture, whether in the education of our best and brightest young people, providing opportunities for underprivileged students, launching the next generation of technical innovation, or establishing the norms and expectations of professional life: in law, medicine, business, communications, and the arts.

Yet today there is a serious loss of trust in universities, as in many other American institutions. To some, they are bastions of elite privilege; to others, centers where ideological conformity threatens freedom of thought. Others see university administrators as self-serving and more interested in boosting institutional reputation rather than in serving students and the public.

It is refreshing to take note of a set of leaders about whom it is hard to be dismissive or cynical. The leaders profiled here uphold and embody the once-cherished ideal that "there are few earthly things more splendid than a university" – in the words of British poet John Masefield (2005). They are all persons of sterling character, exemplars in three respects.

First, they are people whose ambitions were tied to larger purposes, driven by goals higher than self-actualization or material advantage. They share a high degree of commitment and loyalty to the institutions they represent, the colleagues with whom they labor, and all those whom they serve, whether students, clients, patients, athletes, or customers. They seek an institutional context to live out these dreams and commitments.

Second, each of these transformative leaders never lets their personal ambition overwhelm their commitment to people. Without exception, they are committed to creating cultures in which everyone can flourish regardless of rank or position. For every example of them generating new programs and achieving new goals, there are stories of students counseled, young professionals mentored, and employees nurtured. None of these leaders are perfect, to be sure, but their transformative leadership always manifests a humane dimension. People are taken seriously.

The lives of these leaders reflect a commitment to quality without pretension. Few started at the top of the American social order. Reinemund was raised by a single mother who struggled financially. Lamb and Tiefenthaler grew up on farms. After college, Nanni gave himself to work among the poor in Latin America. Woo and Affleck-Graves immigrated to the United States; Chan was the son of immigrants. Freischlag and Walton brought an outsider's view when they achieved positions in elite higher education. Gillespie, a scholar of sterling accomplishment, never relinquished her profound commitment to students. To the rough and tumble of business, Flow brought – of all things – theological conviction. Clawson and White began their athletic vocations at modest institutions, far from the power centers in college athletics.

Their own stories help them avoid the kind of smug elitism that can tarnish higher education. Few of them ever defer to credentials or pedigree. They relish talent and commitment from whatever quarter and actually enjoy nurturing those who did have privilege and connections. Freischlag recounted that when she became chair of surgery at Johns Hopkins, the department was only considering residents from Ivy League institutions. She pointed to a huge stack of rejected applications and exclaimed: "Tell me there is no superb quality there!"

Finally, these leaders are institution builders who infuse character into their respective organizations. This is the most heartening thing about the impact of these leaders. Institutional cultures are being reshaped in ways that bring reality closer to professed ideals. That institutional legacy – a priceless endowment – is the greatest gift these transformative leaders have bestowed.

References

A Note on Sources

In writing these profiles, much depended on my own memories of working with these leaders day in and day out. I also drew upon their own presentations and writings and articles written about them. Using Zoom technology, Mary Pugel and I also undertook scores of interviews with the leaders themselves and with many colleagues and associates, those who could offer firsthand accounts of their leadership. Transcriptions of these interviews have been invaluable.

Introduction

Bennis, W. (1990). *On Becoming a Leader.* Basic Books.
Brant, J., Brooks, E., & Lamb, M. (Eds.). (2022). *Cultivating Virtue in the University.* Oxford University Press.

1 What Is Transformational Leadership?

The Arbinger Institute (2018). *Leadership and Self-Deception: Getting Out of the Box.* Berrett-Koehler Publishers.
Buckingham, M., & Goodall, A. (2019). The power of hidden teams: The most-engaged employees work together in ways companies don't even realize. *Harvard Business Review* (May 2019). https://hbr.org/2019/05/the-power-of-hidden-teams.
Burns, J. M. (1978). *Leadership.* HarperCollins.
Burns, J. M. (2018). *Transforming Leadership.* Grove Press.
Collins, J. (2001). *Good to Great: Why Some Companies Make the Leap . . . and Others Don't.* Harper Business.
Collins, J. (2005). *Good to Great and the Social Sectors: Why Business Thinking Is Not the Answer.* HarperBusiness.
Duckworth, A. (2016). *Grit: The Power of Passion and Perseverance.* Scribner.
Folger Shakespeare Library (n.d.). *Richard III.* The Folger Shakespeare. Retrieved August 17, 2023, from https://bit.ly/42olcEN.
Frei, F. X., & Morriss, A. (2020). Begin with trust: The first step to becoming a genuinely empowering leader. *Harvard Business Review* (May–June). https://hbr.org/2020/05/begin-with-trust.
Goleman, D. (1995). *Emotional Intelligence: Why It Can Matter More than IQ.* Bantam Books.

Goleman, D. (2004). What makes a leader? *Harvard Business Review* (January 2004). https://hbr.org/2004/01/what-makes-a-leader.

Lombardi, J. V., Craig, D. D., Capaldi, E. D., & Gater, D. S. (2000). *The Top American Research Universities, 2000*. The Center (University of Florida). https://bit.ly/42upWJa.

Pasteur, L., & Vallery-Radot, P. (1939). *Oeuvres de Pasteur*. Masson et cie. www.biodiversitylibrary.org/bibliography/1989.

Shenk, J. W. (2006). *Lincoln's Melancholy: How Depression Challenged a President and Fueled His Greatness*. HarperOne.

Zak, P. J. (2017). The neuroscience of trust: Management behaviors that foster employee engagement. *Harvard Business Review* (January–February 2017). https://hbr.org/2017/01/the-neuroscience-of-trust.

2 Carolyn Woo

[CatholicColleges]. (2016, February 3). Carolyn Woo: 2016 ACCU Presidents' Distinguished Service Award [Video]. YouTube. www.youtube.com/watch?v=C9JCvrA4TsM.

Catholic Relief Services (n.d.). LinkedIn.com. Retrieved April 28, 2023, from https://bit.ly/493vL2w.

Catholic Relief Services (n.d.). *Dr. Carolyn Y. Woo: President and CEO, Catholic Relief Services*. Retrieved February 10, 2023, from www.crs.org/sites/default/files/crs-files/carolyn_woo_bio.pdf.

Elliot, C. (2010, March 4). *Notre Dame undergraduate business ranked No. 1 by Bloomberg BusinessWeek*. Notre Dame News. Retrieved February 10, 2023, from https://bit.ly/4biX3Ud.

University of Notre Dame (n.d.). *Carolyn Woo: Distinguished President's Fellow for Global* Development, *Purdue University*. Kellogg Institute for International Studies. Retrieved February 10, 2023, from https://kellogg.nd.edu/carolyn-woo.

Additional References

Melia, M. Personal communication, September 8, 2022.

Nichols, B. Personal communication, July 11, 2022.

Woo, C. Personal communication, March 22, 2022.

3 John Affleck-Graves

Bauer, C. (2018, January 16). Notre Dame puts finishing touches on $400 million Campus Crossroads project. *South Bend Tribune*. https://bit.ly/42thycT.

Gebhard, M. (2019, May 3). *John Affleck-Graves to retire June 30 after 15 years as EVP (and MVP)*. NDWorks: Campus News for Faculty and Staff. Retrieved April 28, 2023, from https://ndworks.nd.edu/news/evp-john-affleck-graves-retires-june-30/.

Jenkins, J. I., C.S.C. (2011, September 20). *President's annual address to the faculty 2011*. Office of the President – Rev. John I. Jenkins, C.S.C. Retrieved April 28, 2023, from https://bit.ly/3SjmoEM.

Observer Staff Report (2018, August 22). John Affleck-Graves announces retirement as executive vice president of Notre Dame. *The Observer*. https://bit.ly/42HILZv.

University of Notre Dame (n.d.). *AIM – Applied Investment Management: About*. Mendoza College of Business. Retrieved April 28, 2023, from https://aim.nd.edu/about/.

University of Notre Dame (n.d.). *AIM – Applied Investment Management: For Alumni*. Mendoza College of Business. Retrieved April 28, 2023, from https://aim.nd.edu/about/.

University of Notre Dame (n.d.). *John Affleck-Graves*. Mendoza College of Business. Retrieved April 28, 2023, from http://bit.ly/3Ov8iio.

Additional References

Affleck-Graves, J. Personal communication, March 29, 2022.

Cullinan, S. Personal communication, July 14, 2022.

Kidder, M. Personal communication, July 19, 2022.

Roche, M. Personal communication, April 1, 2022.

Seamon, M. Personal communication, July 13, 2022.

4 Louis Nanni

Brown, D. (2011, July 12). *Notre Dame campaign raises $2.014 billion*. Notre Dame News. Retrieved May 5, 2023, from https://news.nd.edu/news/notre-dame-campaign-raises-2-014-billion/.

MacCready, S. (2020, August 3). *Episode 40: An interview with Lou Nanni, University of Notre Dame: Leadership, handling uncertain times with COVID-19 & the coronavirus pandemic, and inspiring others with your mission*. Retrieved May 5, 2023, from www.thephilanthropypodcast.com/transcripts-episode-40.

McDonald, C. (2016, April 13). *Homeless by the Dome*. Scholastic. https://scholastic.nd.edu/issues/homeless-by-the-dome/.

Moore, D. (2002, May 2). *Nanni elected vice president for university relations*. Notre Dame News. Retrieved May 5, 2023, from https://news.nd.edu/news/nanni-elected-vice-president-for-university-relations/.

Russell, J. (2022, January 21). *Notre Dame pulls in eight-figure gifts in 2021, adding to a strong fundraising history.* Retrieved May 5, 2023, from www .ibj.com/articles/landing-gold.

University of Notre Dame (n.d.). *Louis M. Nanni: Vice president for university relations.* University of Notre Dame: University Leadership. Retrieved May 5, 2023, from www.nd.edu/about/leadership/council/louis-nanni/.

Additional References

Christophersen, H. Personal communication, July 13, 2022.

Cullinan, S. Personal communication, July 14, 2022.

Kidder, M. Personal communication, July 19, 2022.

Malloy, E., C.S.C. Personal interview, July 15, 2022.

Nanni, L. Personal communication, July 23, 2022.

5 Kevin White

Athletic Coast Conference (n.d.). *James J. Phillips, Ph.D.* ACC Staff. Retrieved May 12, 2023, from https://theacc.com/staff.aspx?staff=84.

Duke University (n.d.). *Kevin White.* Senior Administration. Retrieved May 12, 2023, from https://goduke.com/sports/senior-administration/roster/coaches/kevin-white/2615.

Duke University (n.d.). *Nina King.* Staff Directory. Retrieved May 12, 2023, from https://goduke.com/staff-directory/nina-king/486.

Duke University, Fuqua School of Business (n.d.). *Kevin White, Professor of the Practice and Vice President/Director of Athletics, Emeritus.* Faculty: Kevin White. Retrieved May 12, 2023, from www.fuqua.duke.edu/faculty/kevin-white.

Finkelstein, S. (2016). *Superbosses: How exceptional leaders master the flow of talent.* Portfolio.

Liberty University (n.d.). *Ian McCaw.* Staff. Retrieved May 12, 2023, from www.liberty.edu/flames/staff/ian-mccaw/.

Marquette University (n.d.). *Bill Scholl.* Staff Directory. Retrieved May 12, 2023, from https://gomarquette.com/staff-directory/bill-scholl/2.

National Collegiate Athletic Association (n.d.). *Stan Wilcox: EVP of regulatory affairs at NCAA.* About. Retrieved May 12, 2023, from https://theorg.com/org/national-collegiate-athletic-association/org-chart/stan-wilcox.

North Carolina State University (n.d.). *Boo Corrigan.* Staff Directory. Retrieved May 12, 2023, from https://gopack.com/staff-directory/boo-corrigan/2752.

Notre Dame University (2000, March 13). *Kevin White named new athletic director.* General. Retrieved May 12, 2023, from https://und.com/genrel-031300aaa-html/.

Pennsylvania State University (2022, March 16). *Vice President for Intercollegiate Athletics Sandy Barbour to retire*. General News. Retrieved May 12, 2023, from https://gopsusports.com/news/2022/3/16/general-sandy-barbour-to-retire.aspx.

Stanford University (n.d.). *Bernard Muir: The Jaquish & Kenninger Director of Athletics*. Stanford Athletics. Retrieved May 12, 2023, from https://gostanford.com/staff-directory/bernard-muir/37.

University of California (2013, July 18). *Sandy Barbour bio*. The University of California Official Athletic Site. Retrieved May 12, 2023, from https://calbears.com/sports/2013/4/17/208204079.aspx.

University of North Carolina (2022, July 1). *Bubba Cunningham: Director of Athletics*. University of North Carolina Staff. Retrieved May 12, 2023, from https://goheels.com/staff-directory/bubba-cunningham/1.

Additional References

Cunningham, B. Personal communication, June 29, 2022.

King, N. Personal communication, July 7, 2022.

Muir, B. Personal communication, July 7, 2022.

Phillips, J. Personal communication, July 6, 2022.

White, K. Personal communication, May 22, 2022.

6 Jill Tiefenthaler

The Colorado Springs Business Journal (2014, September 23). *Colorado Colleges receives $5 million donation for library*. Daily News. Retrieved May 12, 2023, from https://bit.ly/3SM8ufZ.

Hanna, V. (2020, April 1). *From building on the block to exploring the planet*. Bulletin. Retrieved May 12, 2023, from https://bit.ly/48RZAmB.

National Geographic Society (2020, August 6). *Meet Jill Tiefenthaler, National Geographic Society's first female chief executive officer*. National Geographic Society Newsroom. Retrieved May 12, 2023, from https://bit.ly/3udln9o.

National Geographic Society (n.d.). *Jill Tiefenthaler*. Our Leadership. www.nationalgeographic.org/society/our-leadership/.

Shakespeare, W. (2001). *The tragedy of king Richard III*. Oxford Paperbacks.

Additional References

Chan, E. Personal communication, August 30, 2022.

Davis, J. Personal communication, August 22, 2022.

Matthews, R. Personal communication, August 15, 2022.

Sutton, L. Personal communication, August 16, 2022.

Tiefenthaler, J. Personal communication, March 30, 2022.

7 Steve Reinemund

Anderson, M. (2013, November 1). *Determination and a dream*. Wake Forest News. Retrieved May 12, 2023, from https://news.wfu.edu/2013/11/01/deter mination-and-a-dream/.

Fyten, D. (Winter 2008). *The head has a heart*. Wake Forest Magazine Archive. Retrieved May 12, 2023, from https://archive.magazine.wfu.edu/winter-2008/the-head-has-a-heart/.

Halpern, T. (n.d.). *Steven S Reinemund, 1948–*. Business Biographies. www .referenceforbusiness.com/biography/M-R/Reinemund-Steven-S-1948.html.

Henson, M. (2011, January 20). Honor thy father: Mike and Mary Farrell's historic gift is a tribute to their family's past and an investment in Wake Forest's future. *Wake Forest Magazine* (Spring 2011), 18–23. https://maga zine.wfu.edu/2011/01/20/honor-thy-father/.

Steven Reinemund. (2023, April 8). Wikipedia. https://en.wikipedia.org/wiki/ Steven_Reinemund.

Wake Forest University School of Business (2008, April 22). *Former PepsiCo CEO Reinemund named business dean*. The Newsroom. Retrieved May 12, 2023, from https://bit.ly/485zP11.

Wake Forest University School of Business (2013, September 19). *Record turnout for Dawn with the Dean*. The Newsroom. https://business.wfu.edu/ newsroom/record-turnout-dawn-with-dean/.

Wake Forest University School of Business (n.d.). *Master of Science in Management Program*. Masters in Management. Retrieved May 12, 2023, from https://business.wfu.edu/masters-in-management/.

[YouTube]. (2014, November 20). *The last lecture: An evening with Steve Reinemund* [Video]. Wake Forest University School of Business. www .youtube.com/watch?v=7_j8-oag5qc.

Additional References

Dupree, D. Personal communication, August 18, 2022.

Iacovou, C. Personal communication, August 19, 2022.

Johnson, T. Personal communication, August 22, 2022.

8 Andy Chan

Chan, A. (2010). Life after college. *Wake Forest Magazine* (Spring 2010). https://archive.magazine.wfu.edu/spring-2010/life-after-college/.

Chan, A., & Derry, T. (2013). A roadmap for transforming the college-to-career experience. *Rethinking success: From the liberal arts to career in the 21st century*. https://bit.ly/486obCO.

Dominus, S. (2013, September 13). How to get a job with a philosophy degree. *New York Times Magazine*, MM40. https://bit.ly/3Us0fGQ.

Duke Divinity (2013, July 1). *Andy Chan: Thinking holistically about careers.* Faith & Leadership. Retrieved May 18, 2023, from https://faithandleader ship.com/andy-chan-thinking-holistically-about-careers.

Madden, S. (2012, April 29). *Recommendations.* LinkedIn. Retrieved August 17, 2023, from www.linkedin.com/in/chanfucious/.

[TEDx Talks]. (2013, May 13). *"Career services" must die: Andy Chan at TEDxLawrenceU* [Video]. YouTube. www.youtube.com/watch?v=6Tc6GH WPdMU.

Wake Forest University (2022, July 14). *About the School of Professional Studies.* School of Professional Studies. Retrieved May 18, 2023, from https://sps.wfu.edu/articles/about-us/.

Wake Forest University (n.d.). *Expert: Andy Chan.* Wake Forest News. Retrieved May 18, 2023, from https://news.wfu.edu/expert-profiles/andy-chan/.

Wake Forest University (n.d.). *Help private companies build better business.* Wake Forest University Center for Private Business. Retrieved May 18, 2023, from https://cpb.wfu.edu/.

Wake Forest University (n.d.). *Office of Personal and Career Development.* About the OPCD. Retrieved May 18, 2023, from https://opcd.wfu.edu/about-the-opcd/.

Additional References

Chan, A. Personal communication, March, 30, 2022.

Derry, T. Personal communication, November 17, 2022.

Eyadiel, M. Personal communication, October 17, 2022.

Laws, K. Personal communication, November 8, 2022.

McWilliams, A. Personal communication, October 12, 2022.

Robinson, H. Personal communication, October 20, 2022.

Selverian, M. personal communication, November 29, 2022.

9 Michele Gillespie

King, K. M. (2004, June 1). Southern accent: Students can recite Michele K. Gillespie's philosophy in unison: History is what people remember and why they remember it the way they do. *Wake Forest Magazine*.

Neal, K. (2017, August 18). *"This is perfect": WFU launches engineering program enriched by liberal arts.* Wake Forest News. Retrieved May 15, 2023, from https://bit.ly/4boQKhO.

Wake Forest University (n.d.). *The Environmental Program*. Center for Energy, Environment and Sustainability. Retrieved May 15, 2023, from https://cees .wfu.edu/academics/the-environmental-program/.

Wake Forest University (n.d.). *Our history*. The Program for Leadership and Character. Retrieved May 15, 2023, from https://leadershipandcharacter.wfu .edu/vision-2/our-history/.

Wake Forest University (n.d.). *Welcome from the Dean of the College*. Wake Forest College of Arts and Sciences. Retrieved May 15, 2023, from https:// college.wfu.edu/welcome-dean-college/.

Walker, C. (2017, January 10). *Classes begin at Wake Downtown, Wake Forest's urban campus*. Wake Forest News. Retrieved May 15, 2023, from https://bit .ly/49n2C2c.

Additional References

Alexander, R. Personal communication, January 12, 2023.

Colyer, C. Personal communication, January 23, 2023.

Gillespie, M. Personal communication, January 5, 2023.

Marsh, A. Personal communication, January 19, 2023.

Matthews, R. Personal communication, January 17, 2023.

Morgan, J. R. Personal communication, January 30, 2023.

10 Julie Freischlag

American College of Surgeons (2021, November 1). *Julie A. Freischlag, MD, FACS, FRCSEd(Hon), DFSVS, installed as President of the ACS*. Bulletin of the American College of Surgeons. Retrieved May 18, 2023, from https://bit.ly/4bADcjw.

Atrium Health Wake Forest Baptist (n.d.). *Julie A. Freischlag, MD, FACS, FRCSEd (Hon), DFSVS, MAMSE*. Leadership. Retrieved May 18, 2023, from www.wakehealth.edu/about-us/leadership/freischlag.

Berger, C., & Faria, P. (2020, October 9). *Atrium Health and Wake Forest Baptist Health combine, create next-generation academic health system*. Atrium Health News. https://bit.ly/3SpadGE.

Berger, C., Faria, P., & Eaton, B. (2019, April 10). *Atrium Health, Wake Forest Baptist Health and Wake Forest University announce intent to create transformative academic healthcare system*. Atrium Health News. Retrieved May 18, 2023, from https://atriumhealth.org/about-us/newsroom/news/ 2019/04/best-care-for-all.

Buechner, F. (1973). *Wishful thinking: A seeker's ABC*. HarperCollins.

Carolina Panthers (n.d.). *InspiHER, presented by Atrium Health: Episode 207 with Julie A. Freischlag.* InspiHER Podcast. Retrieved May 18, 2023, from https://bit.ly/49n31Sg.

Davis, J. (2017, April 28). *Wake Forest's epic EHR rollout was a money pit. Here's how they turned it around.* https://bit.ly/486otcS.

Merisow, A., & Berger, C. (2022, December 2). *Advocate Aurora Health and Atrium Health complete combination.* Atrium Health News. Retrieved May 18, 2023, from https://bit.ly/3HKQbBh.

Minemyer, P. (2017, September 1). *UNC Health Care, Carolinas HealthCare System to merge and form one of the country's largest nonprofit systems.* Finance. Retrieved May 18, 2023, from https://bit.ly/481BsNe.

Minemyer, P. (2018, March 2). *Atrium Health suspends merger talks with UNC Health Care.* Finance. Retrieved May 18, 2023, from https://bit.ly/3w4G5sw.

Society of University Surgeons (2022, January 28). *The SUS is pleased to honor the 2021 Trailblazer Award Winner Julie A. Freischlag, MD, FACS, FRCSEd(Hon), DFSVS.* 2021 Trailblazer Award Winner: Julie A. Freischlag, MD, FACS, FRCSEd(Hon), DFSVS. Retrieved May 18, 2023, from https://bit.ly/49gNns1.

Additional References

Freischlag, J. Personal communication, July 12, 2022.

Freischlag, J. Personal communication, May 8, 2023.

Gibel, A. Personal communication, January 20, 2023.

High, K. Personal communication, January 25, 2023.

Tuttle, B. Personal communication, February 1, 2023.

Wallace, M. Personal communication, January 25, 2023.

Warden, W. Personal communication, January 24, 2023.

11 Jonathan Lee Walton

Batten, M., & Walker, C. (2019, April 28). *Jonathan L. Walton named Dean of the School of Divinity.* School of Divinity. Retrieved July 14, 2023, from https://bit.ly/3Su6JTe.

Harvard University (n.d.). *Professor Jonathan L. Walton.* Harvard – The Memorial Church. Retrieved July 14, 2023, from https://memorialchurch.harvard.edu/sermons-jonathan-l-walton.

Henson, M. (2020, October 5). "One Luv": Jonathan Walton (D.D. '15), dean of the School of Divinity, calls us to bear witness in these times. *Wake Forest Magazine* (Fall). https://magazine.wfu.edu/2020/10/05/one-luv/.

Lischer, R. (1997). *The preacher king: Martin Luther King, Jr. and the word that moved America*. Oxford University Press. https://bit.ly/3HRgkyg.

Morehouse College (n.d.). *Lawrence Edward Carter Sr.* Humanities, Social Sciences, Media and Arts Division Faculty. Retrieved July 14, 2023, from https://morehouse.edu/carter-lawrence-e/.

Wake Forest University (n.d.). *COMPASS Initiative Faith Coordinating Center*. School of Divinity. Retrieved July 14, 2023, from https://divinity.wfu.edu/compass-initiative-faith-coordinating-center/.

Walton, J. L. (2015, May 29). *Benediction* [Prayer at Commencement]. Harvard University. https://bit.ly/4bse3Y0.

Walton, J. L. (2018, January 30). *Laying our hammers down* [Morning Chapel]. Harvard University. www.youtube.com/watch?v=ZbTrhKpx2k8.

Walton, J. L. (2018, January 31). *The inconvenience of truth* [Sermon]. Harvard University. https://memorialchurch.harvard.edu/blog/inconvenience-truth.

Walton, J. L. (2018, September 5). *Looking at life through a lens of love* [Morning Chapel]. Harvard University. https://memorialchurch.harvard.edu/blog-categories/morning-prayers?page=2.

Additional References

Faust, D. Personal communication, April 11, 2023.

Gray, N. Personal communication, April 17, 2023.

Leonard, B. Personal communication, April 17, 2023.

Morgan, R. Personal communication, May 1, 2023.

Walton, J. Personal communication, May 2, 2023.

Walton, J. Personal communication, August 17, 2023.

12 Michael Lamb

Brant, J., Brooks, E., & Lamb, M. (Eds.). (2022). *Cultivating virtue in the university*. Oxford University Press.

Lamb, M. (2007). Personal statement applying for doctoral studies in political theory at Princeton University.

Lamb, M., Brant, J., & Brooks, E. (2021). How is virtue cultivated? Seven strategies for postgraduate character development. *Journal of Character Education*, *17*(1), 81–108.

Michael Lamb (n.d.). About. Retrieved May 29, 2023, from http://kmichaellamb.com/.

Wake Forest University (n.d.). *Michael Lamb*. The Program for Leadership and Character. Retrieved May 29, 2023, from https://leadershipandcharacter.wfu.edu/michael-lamb/.

Walker, C. (2023, January 24). *Wake Forest University awarded $30M Lilly Endowment Inc. grant to build national capacity for character education*. Wake Forest News. Retrieved May 29, 2023, from https://bit.ly/3Ouxcie.

Additional References

Bryant, D. Personal communication, March 22, 2023.
Gregory, E. Personal communication, April 11, 2023.
Huebner, T. Personal communication, March 28, 2023.
Lamb, M. Personal communication, July 22, 2022.
Lamb, M. Personal communication, March 19, 2023.
Maceto, S. Personal communication, March 21, 2023.
O'Connell, J. Personal communication, March 21, 2023.
Phelps, A. Personal communication, April 4, 2023.
Silverglate, C. Personal communication, March 27, 2023.
Townsend, K. Personal communication, March 17, 2023.

13 Dave Clawson

Associated Press (2013, December 7). *Bowling Green wins MAC title, ruins Northern Illinois' BCS hopes*. College Football Recap. Retrieved May 18, 2023, from www.espn.com/college-football/recap/_/gameId/333402459.

Hale, D. (2021, November 5). *Dave Clawson has created college football version's of Moneyball at Wake Forest*. ESPN College Football. Retrieved May 18, 2023, from https://bit.ly/3SuT12r.

Haney, T. (2015, February 23). *Which jobs are the worst?* ESPN+ College Football Insider. Retrieved May 18, 2023, from https://bit.ly/3Ox5Jwt.

Karp, B. (2022, September 8). Film Room: The infamous Wake Forest slow mesh. *The Vanderbilt Hustler*.

Pantages, W. (2022, November 15). *Wake Forest ties program record with 96 percent graduation success rate*. Wake Forest Athletics News. Retrieved May 18, 2023, from https://bit.ly/4bCZHV5.

Raynor, G. (2023, March 7). *"The Big Short": The secret to Wake Forest's QB success on the recruiting trail*. The Athletic: NCAAF. Retrieved May 18, 2023, from https://theathletic.com/4281771/2023/03/07/wake-forest-recruiting-quarterbacks/.

Staples, A. (2022, October 6). *Dear Andy: Kansas State's stars, Dave Clawson at Wake Forest and media to coaching pipeline*. The Athletic: NCAAF. Retrieved May 18, 2023, from https://bit.ly/4bsqXFI.

Additional References

Clawson, D. Personal communication, June 23, 2022.

Clawson, D. Personal communication, February 16, 2023.

Cohen, D. Personal communication, February 23, 2023.

Dunn, W. Personal communication, March 2, 2023.

Higgins, K. Personal communication, February 23, 2023.

Jarry, J. Personal communication, March 1, 2023.

Wolford, J. Personal communication, February 28, 2023.

14 Don Flow

Bower, J. L., & Paine, L. S. (2017). The error at the heart of corporate leadership. *Harvard Business Review* (May–June 2017). https://bit.ly/3OwmHLv.

Buffett, W., & Munger, C. (2017, June 1). *Warren Buffett and Charlie Munger on auto dealerships*. Focusedcompounding.com. Retrieved August 17, 2023, from https://bit.ly/3SnDz8h.

Duke University Divinity School (2010, February 15). *Don Flow: How do you live faithfully?* Faith & Leadership. Retrieved July 17, 2023, from https://faithandleadership.com/don-flow-how-do-you-live-faithfully.

Erisman, A. M. (2004, April 1). *Don Flow: Ethics at Flow Automotive*. Ethix.org. https://ethix.org/2004/04/01/ethics-at-flow-automotive.

Flow Automotive (n.d.). *About Us*. Retrieved July 17, 2023, from www.flowauto.com/Home/About.

Flow Leadership Philosophy (2005). Internal Memo of Flow Companies LLC.

O'Toole, J. (2019). *The enlightened capitalists: Cautionary tales of business pioneers who tried to do well by doing good*. Harper Business.

Wake Forest University (n.d.). *Distinguished Alumni Award 2017*. Alumni & Friends. Retrieved July 17, 2023, from https://bit.ly/4bnTR9O.

Additional References

Chan, A. Personal communication, April 20, 2023.

Erisman, A. Personal communication, April 21, 2023.

Flow, D. Personal communication, May 25, 2023.

Freischlag, J. Personal communication, May 8, 2023.

Haslam, B. Personal communication, April 26, 2023.

Hunter, J. Personal communication, May 23, 2023.

Johnson, T. Personal communication, April 19, 2023.

Joines, A. Personal communication, April 20, 2023.

Mack, W. Personal communication, July 7, 2023.

Conclusion

Masefield, J. (2005). *Sea-fever: Selected poems of John Masefield* (P. W. Errington, Ed.). Carcanet Press Ltd.

Acknowledgments

Hatch, N. O. (2021, December 15). How to hire leaders better than yourself. *Chronicle of Higher Education*.

Additional References

Freischlag, J. Personal communication, May 8, 2023.

Dedication

The work is dedicated to three priest-scholars who have guided the transformation of Notre Dame over the last seventy years:

- Father Theodore Hesburgh, C.S.C.
- Father Edward A. Malloy, C.S.C.
- Father John I. Jenkins, C.S.C.

And to my friends and colleagues on the president's senior team – who guided Wake Forest University through the crisis of the COVID-19 pandemic with creativity, resolve, and goodwill.

Jane Aiken
Andy Chan
John Currie
Jim Dunn
Michele Gillespie
Charles Iacovou
Todd Johnson
Rogan Kersh
Eric Maguire
Hof Milam
Reid Morgan
Mark Petersen
Mary Pugel
Michelle Roehm
Penny Rue
José Villalba
Jonathan Lee Walton

Acknowledgments

This is an Element that has evolved. I had written an article, drawn from my experience, about the value of going the second mile to recruit talent (Hatch, 2021). Throughout my career, I witnessed the transforming power that leaders could bring in a variety of sectors, and I became intrigued by telling their stories.

I am deeply grateful to each of these colleagues for allowing me to offer a brief sketch of their leadership. In each case, much more could be written.

I trust these focused profiles do no disservice to that richer story. Studying these colleagues only increased my appreciation of their manifold gifts.

I am also thankful for the generous assistance of Mary Pugel and Elaine Tooley. Both were great colleagues in envisioning the project and carrying it forward. On the front end, Mary played a crucial role in conducting many of the interviews on which these profiles are based. Elaine is a great stylist and editor and did much to prune and polish my prose. Working with them on this project has been a real joy.

Cambridge Elements ⚌

Leadership

Ronald E. Riggio
Claremont McKenna College

Ronald E. Riggio, Ph.D., is the Henry R. Kravis Professor of Leadership and Organisational Psychology and former Director of the Kravis Leadership Institute at Claremont McKenna College. Dr. Riggio is a psychologist and leadership scholar with over a dozen authored or edited books and more than 150 articles/book chapters. He has worked as a consultant and serves on multiple editorial boards.

Susan E. Murphy
University of Edinburgh

Susan E. Murphy is Chair in Leadership Development at the University of Edinburgh Business School. She has published numerous articles and book chapters on leadership, leadership development, and mentoring. Susan was formerly Director of the School of Strategic Leadership Studies at James Madison University and Professor of Leadership Studies. Prior to that, she served as faculty and associate director of the Henry R. Kravis Leadership Institute at Claremont McKenna College. She also serves on the editorial board of *The Leadership Quarterly*.

Georgia Sorenson
University of Cambridge

The late Georgia Sorenson, Ph.D., was the James MacGregor Burns Leadership Scholar at the Moller Institute and Moller By-Fellow of Churchill College at Cambridge University. Before coming to Cambridge, she founded the James MacGregor Burns Academy of Leadership at the University of Maryland, where she was Distinguished Research Professor. An architect of the leadership studies field, Dr. Sorenson has authored numerous books and refereed journal articles.

About the series

Cambridge Elements in Leadership is multi- and inter-disciplinary and will have broad appeal for leadership courses in Schools of Business, Education, Engineering, and Public Policy and in the Social Sciences and Humanities.

Cambridge Elements ☰

Leadership

Elements in the series

A full series listing is available at: www.cambridge.org/CELE

Printed in the United States
by Baker & Taylor Publisher Services